THE LAWN

Dedicated to groundsmen and greenkeepers everywhere who toil against drought, frost, flood, poaceous pestilence and the tread of corpulent members who have no intention of ever replacing a divot.

THE LAWN

Peter Macinnis

PIER
9

CONTENTS

Introduction   8

1. The origins of the modern lawn   24

2. Means, motive and opportunity
   come together   44

3. Parks, gardens and grandeur   62

4. The lawn imperative   80

5. Lawn, status and authority   98

6. Defending the lawn   116

7. Chemical warfare   134

8. The rise of the mower   152

9. Powered mowers   172

10. Fun on the lawn   192

11. The rise and fall of the
    professional lawn   212

PETER MACINNIS, science writer and broadcaster, has worked in museums, taught in schools, and written for online encyclopaedias. He is now a full-time writer. Among his many publications are *Bittersweet, the story of sugar* (Allen & Unwin 2002); *Rockets* (Allen & Unwin 2003); *The Killer Bean of Calabar, the story of poisons and poisoners* (Allen & Unwin 2004) which was published by Arcade in the US as *Poisons*, and has been translated into Polish, Slovak and Russian; *Kokoda Track: 101 Days* (Black Dog Books 2007) which was short-listed for the New South Wales Premier's History Awards in 2007, and was also an Eve Pownall Honour Book in the 2008 Children's Book Council of Australia Book of the Year Awards; *Pioneers, Heroes and Fools* (Murdoch Books 2007); *Mr Darwin's Incredible Shrinking World* (Murdoch Books 2008); *The Speed of Nearly Everything* (Murdoch Books 2008); and *100 Discoveries* (Murdoch Books 2009).

INTRODUCTION

It is a cliché of crime fiction that the criminal lurking in a group of suspects is the one (there is only ever one!) person who has the means, the opportunity and the motive. Real life can be more complex but the lawn, which some would call a crime, was only possible when the means (the lawn mower) met the opportunity (the open space and leisure time to cultivate a lawn) and the motive (a firm belief that lawn owners would be seen to have 'arrived').

In this book, I explore the strange coming-together of means, opportunity and motive in the mid-nineteenth century, and the lasting social changes that followed when the lawn emerged as the dominant slice of the modern built environment. After the lawn, leisure time would never be the same.

The key enabling technology, the device that made things possible, the invention that let grass dominate our environment was the lawn mower. Without the mower, the emerging professional middle class might admire the lawns of the aristocracy, but lawns remained out of reach to people who could not command the efforts of a veritable army of menial servants, armed with scythes and directing grazing animals.

Even with the mower in place, lawn could only impose itself on ordinary citizens as an object of veneration and a source of toil when the suburbs provided enough space for lawn to fit. The enabling technology that in turn allowed suburbs to exist was commuter transport. Stately homes and city parks could have lawns without transport, because the aristocrats did not

need to go to an office each day, and even if they did, their servants were on site all day. Moving wealthy professional people out to homes with space meant developing accessible suburbs with houses on separate blocks. Only suburbs gave enough space between and around the houses for lawns to fit.

Lawn mowers and suburbs would not have been enough to drive the lawn craze if people had not firmly believed that ownership of a lawn was proof that the owner was a person of status. Or to be blunt, that a lawn owner was rich. In order to prove how rich they were, people were willing to waste their leisure time, were happy to pillage and devastate the environment and they were eager to squander their wealth to show that they really *were* wealthy.

I first put pen to paper on this work in August 2008. In reality, there was no pen and no paper, just the gentle glow of white print on the dark blue screen of my word processor. It seems to be always our habit to look to the past for phrases to describe what we do today.

For example, take the word 'mow', from the Old English *máwan*, which is usually taken to mean 'to cut with a scythe'. It relates to an old Germanic root, *me-*, which we see in words like meadow and mead (the land-form, not the drink). These are fields that are regularly mown to take crops of hay. Today, the word 'mow' has been subverted, stolen away to be used only for non-agricultural purposes.

One advantage of using my word processor to write is that I can go back and look at the date-prints on files to work out when I started writing a book. In the same way I can (and often need to) look at the dates of emails to friends. By these, I can deduce when the idea for this or that book first came to me. This one began in late 2006, when I began digging (like lawns, books involve a lot of digging). This time, I know without looking when I started turning my notes to text. It was 8 August 2008 or 08/08/08, the day the Olympic Games began in Beijing. It was, we were told, an auspicious date in Chinese numerology.

The day 08/08/08 struck me as an appropriate day to start. I had no theory about lucky and unlucky numbers, but there was a definite resonance between lawns and Olympic Games. It was nothing to do with the 2000 Sydney Olympics opening ceremony, where the rotary mower, known to Australians as the 'Victa', an item which has a long held iconic status on the island continent, featured somewhat tongue-in-cheekily. That was a side issue. The true link was the turning of grass into lawn.

The Olympic Games of the twenty-first century, like those of the twentieth century, have been filled with fine examples of our modern obsession with running, jumping, throwing things and forming small packs to pursue harmless spheres. This whole range of human endeavour has largely arisen as the logical aftermath of a simple nineteenth century invention, the lawn mower. It is true that some of the summer Olympic sports take place indoors, in water (or in beach volleyball, on sand). It is equally clear that shooting and cycling are largely independent of grass or lawns, although archery is still a grass sport. All the same, the world's most popular spectator sports seem to be those played on carefully prepared grassy fields, or on artful surrogates for turf.

These games were all *originally* played on grass, on blemished surfaces that we would now dismiss as less suitable for play than for a cow yard. Without the lawn mower and the tireless pursuit of smoother, truer playing surfaces, the modern Olympics would not be what they are. No scythe, no sickle, no herd of animals could deliver the greens, the courts and the fields that we have come to expect for our games.

I am like Rudyard Kipling's Elephant's Child. I enjoy pursuing temporary obsessions. I follow simple facts and curious side issues down burrows, I track them across plains, and I chase them up trees. I go wherever they lead, wherever they hide. I do this to find explanations and origins for things, and then I share the interesting bits I have unearthed. In the technical language of the literati, I write narrative non-fiction, but I prefer to think of it as writing the histories of things.

In one recent case, the 'thing' was not an object or a commodity but the year 1859, and all of the unusual events that took place in that year. There were some pretty patterns waiting to be found, and I was surprised to see how many sports had their origins within a year or two either side of that year. I began to wonder what trigger led to this blossoming of sports played on grass or lawn.

THE ADVANCE OF TECHNOLOGY

While I pursue many temporary obsessions, I can find time for only one permanent obsession. That involves the way we can never predict the social effects of any technology when it is invented. In fact, those effects do not generally begin to appear until about 30 years after an invention, and they remain less than clear until 50 years after the invention was first set loose in public.

It is probably no coincidence that the books produced in the first 50 years after Johannes Gutenberg started using the printing press are called *incunabula,* a term that refers to the clothing of infants. It was only after one full human working life that the idea of printing had been taken on board by both scholars and the people in the printing trade; it had become a mature technology.

After 20 years, people generally know about a new technology, after 30 years, it is growing popular but still developing. After 50 years, we can call it mature. It does not matter if you look at printing, the telescope, the telegraph, the railway, photography, radio, television, cinema, heavier-than-air flight or the internet. Within a tolerance of a few years, the 30-year/50-year effect holds in every case. The duration is probably linked to the working lifespan of human beings, but whatever the cause, the effect is common.

Back in 1459, Gutenberg could not have anticipated two books published 400 years on, in 1859, Charles Darwin's *The Origin of Species* and Charles Dickens' *A Tale of Two Cities*—or their effects. Gutenberg was content to have a system that could produce 180 bibles in the time that one diligent penman could complete a single copy by hand. He could never have imagined that in Mainz in 2008, outside a museum devoted to his work, daily newspapers from many nations would be sold to foreign tourists. Museums, newspapers, tourists and flying would have made no sense to him at all.

The Wright brothers in 1903 knew about newspapers, but they couldn't have foreseen air-freighting them between continents, or a tourist trade powered by cheap and fast air travel. The inventors of the first primitive internet connections in 1969 couldn't have predicted that those same tourists would book their flights, hotels and entertainment, online. The internet still has a few of its allotted maturation years left, and even now, we cannot predict with certainty where it will lead, though we can see some signs. It is possible that the future may see Mr Gutenberg's invention somewhat eclipsed as more text is placed online, or as print-on-demand takes over, but for the most part, we don't know what's coming. We can't know what's coming.

Marshall McLuhan made the point that our descriptions of new technologies are always based on what we know from the past, so I still talk of setting pen to paper, people in the early twentieth century drove horseless carriages, sent messages by wireless telegraphy and watched moving pictures—and we send carbon copies of emails and mow lawns. I wonder what scythe operators in 1808 would have made of the effects of the lawn mower. Could they have predicted the media circus and loss of work time that constitutes the games of any modern Olympiad?

Legend has it that Niels Bohr said 'Prediction is difficult—especially about the future'. Bohr claimed that somebody else said it, but the statement remains true. Logical consequences only look logical when we view them from the other side, when we can see which scraps of context really counted. Even Arthur C. Clarke (who predicted communications satellites in 1945) never saw the full potential when he wrote that first outline.

The internet began in 1969, and jumped a notch when the world wide web began in 1989. By 2004, it was established and understood by most of the civilised world but it was still expanding. Now the world is dotted with internet cafes that allow the world traveller to stay connected, and wifi points allow the laptop carrier to remain enmeshed in the web, 24/7. To return to the core theme, some of the most pleasant hot spots are in parks with lawns, like the area adjacent to the New York Public Library in Bryant Park or the seven zones (at last count) in New York's Central Park. What else will change by 2019?

There is a good reason why we cannot predict the social effects of a new technology nor which will be successful. Each technology grows and develops its surprising new applications in a sea of other technologies, and there are just too many combinations, permutations, chances for surprises.

The first railway opened in 1830. By 1855, most nations had at least a small railroad either opened or planned. By 1870, railways had been used in both the US Civil War and the Franco-Prussian War. By 1880, Europe, North America and Australia were all criss-crossed by rail lines, and railways had brought the world closer together.

Thanks to commuter rail lines, cities developed suburbs in the mid-1800s, from which workers could commute each day. Rail transport got them home quickly to spacious blocks of land which gave them all a place to grow things in their leisure time. Nobody could have predicted that effect.

It must have been a fine thing to develop a better way of rigging a ship or a technique for defending hulls against the attacks of hungry worms. No matter what the promise of those inventions, without a decent compass, without somebody building a better chronometer to allow the calculation of longitude, without some keen medical observer explaining the causes of scurvy, the shipbuilding innovations could go nowhere, because the ships could not be sailed with any certainty, and because the crews died before they got anywhere.

So with no criticism of Edwin Budding, this is the story of the many unpredicted and unanticipated effects of his adaptation in 1830 of a small cloth-improving tool to make the first lawn mower. In an act that would have astounded the original inventor, he modified a tool so it could mow grass and accidentally triggered our modern sports-mad era. By 1860, the mower was a largely mature technology, and its social effects were becoming apparent as we found new ways to use our smooth new lawns. The lawn mower changed our society.

So what inspired Budding's starting point, what made somebody build the tool that inspired the lawn mower? I found the answer on a wall in the Netherlands, in a museum I was visiting because it had a supply of Rembrandts and because it seemed like a good idea at the time.

THE LEIDEN CONNECTION

My wife and I always set out early for towns with unusual museums. While this helps us avoid crowds, it has its drawbacks. In 2004, the efficiently helpful SNCF staff at Gare Saint-Lazare in Paris took us in hand and bundled us onto a speedy train earlier than the slow service we had planned. The result was our arrival in Le Havre, three hours before our target museum opened.

It was a chilly, windy and rainy day in late April, more winter than summer. We wandered, buffeted this way and that, through a town where unseen workers above us scrubbed seagull excrement from buildings. To dodge the spray of lime-rich, fish-stinking splatters, we took refuge in a tavern. Later, we were told that it was the epicentre of the red light district.

We were drawn to the tavern because it was on the corner of two streets, each bearing the name of an early French voyager to Australia. The other customers seemed to be extras from *Irma La Douce*, but it suffices to note that they were probably professionally qualified for such roles. They welcomed us as fellow humans on a cold day.

On an allegedly summer day in 2008, we found ourselves in Leiden early on a Sunday morning. This Netherlands university town is remarkably compact, but even if things were all close together, they were also closed. The cafes and bars were shut, and contrary to what our guidebook said, the promised early-opening exhibitions were yet to unlock their doors.

So we circled the chilly, windy streets around the Stedelijk Museum De Lakenhal until it opened at noon, our tongues hanging out for a coffee. Recollections of Le Havre ducked and weaved through our teeth-chattering discussions, but in the end, it was worth going to Leiden, if only because I found the ancestor of the lawn mower.

The Lakenhal museum offers a wealth of fine art without the crowds of larger museums and it commemorates the building's history. It offers an insight into a time when Leiden depended on cloth making, the world depended on Leiden cloth and the Lakenhal was the centre of power among the cloth makers of Leiden. We went there mainly for the art, but in one room, I spotted a large implement, about 150 cm (five feet) long with two heavy iron arms joined by a spring. One of the arms was seriously weighted and each arm had a cutting edge. The implement was just slung on a wall.

The object had no explanatory text, but I knew immediately what it was; I had read about shears like this. These shears were once used to remove the nap (or knap), the rough bits, from a length of cloth. They were huge, heavy and, if left in the hands of the untrained, inclined to damage the cloth.

Keep in mind that with the onset of the industrial revolution, the English were rather big in the textiles industry as well. They were very good at it, and in the early nineteenth century, they were also becoming very good at making machines to do most of the hard work.

There were machines for preparing and spinning the yarn, machines to weave the threads into cloth, and there were machines that napped (or knapped) the cloth, clearing away any rough and lumpy surface bits that spoiled the feel of the fabric. Napping or knapping shears like the ones on the wall in Leiden.

Some cloths make a feature of nap, the sort of texture that comes from having a raised pile: terry cloth, chenille and velvet all have a nap (and it's seen as a plus). Worsted also has nap, but on this cloth, nap is undesirable, so worsted is trimmed. Once, humans did this work with huge shears like the ones before me. These were skilled workers who wore fancy shirts with frilled fronts with sleeves held above the elbows by pieces of scarlet cloth. It took practice and craft to not make holes in the cloth as it was trimmed, so the operators were proud of their skill, and they commanded respect.

They stretched the cloth over a special board with weights, and then laid the monster shears weighing 20–40 kg (around 50 pounds) on the cloth. The English shearmen used a block of lead to keep the shears close to the work. Operating the shears was tiring, and often a strong boy was 'colted' to learn the job. Once colted, he was then exploited for an apprenticeship of three or four years to do most of the lifting of the weights. Then the boy was free to set up on his own, and in time, engage his own colt.

The shears must have been valuable. In 1764, the Surrey Quarter Sessions heard a case against Thomas Cooley and John Fleming who faced a charge of stealing from James Kilvington's Knapping Mill in Gravel Lane, Southwark. They were accused of having taken '2 pieces of lead called the riders for the knapping shears, containing in weight about 40 pounds', along with three small brass boxes, and of selling them, together with three iron bolts.

The Leiden shears would have been cheaper than their English equivalents, but harder to use. They had the weights built in as a slab of iron, but there could be no doubting their intended purpose. The shears were heavy and brutal, looking more like an instrument designed to snip fingers, ears, noses, toes and other protruding bits. They scarcely resembled a precision instrument that might be wielded with skill, but they were undoubtedly napping shears, and at one stage, the best available. With practice, a skilled worker could wield the shears reliably and earn good money.

Then in 1815, John Lewis patented a small device in England that anybody, even the unskilled, could use. It could be rolled across the cloth, with no fear of harming the weavers' work. It was a napping machine, based on a slightly older American design. The British shearmen disliked this machine because it made untrained workers their equals. Still, the Lewis cutters did rather well.

Some time later, Lewis came up with an improved device. Now, because this is the story about the role of the lawn mower in shaping our society, you probably won't be too surprised to know that Lewis' new version looked and worked rather like a small manual push mower, the sort that has a spinning cylinder of blades. The sort that lops off the longer stems and blades of grass and beheads the weeds.

Lewis' cutter was faster and lighter than shears, and did a slightly poorer job but, like the earlier version, it saved the shearmen from repetitive strain injuries. Though the devices were expensive, unskilled workers with the money for a Lewis cutter could earn a living. Working a twelve-hour day on piece-rates, an operator could pay for his machine in a year. In time, the price of a cutter dropped and it became more affordable. In the long run, these machines displaced the skilled operators with their frilly shirts and sleeves held up with scarlet ties.

The sum effect of all of the machines brought into the textile trade would be that workers everywhere could earn a living wage, mill owners could turn a nice profit, and everybody could have more leisure time. But as we have long warned each other, the devil makes work for idle hands. In this case, the work came in the form of a neat but enlarged version of the napping machine, manufactured at the Phoenix Ironworks of John Ferrabee, located at Thrupp in England's Gloucestershire. It was destined to eat a lot of precious leisure time.

The early napping machines had a straight blade, but soon a helical blade, a twisted blade just like the ones seen on cylinder lawn mowers today, replaced this. Then in May 1830, Edwin Beard Budding, an ingenious man who may or may not have been one of Ferrabee's employees, had an idea. He asked: why not make it bigger, add a handle, and use it to mow grass? Ferrabee liked the idea and the two men soon reached a financial agreement about making the new machine and sharing the profits. On 25 October 1830, Budding obtained a patent on 'a new combination and application of machinery for the purpose of cropping or shearing the vegetable surfaces of lawns, grass-plats, and pleasure grounds, constituting a machine which may be used with advantage instead of a scythe for that purpose'.

One of the earliest models was tested at the Regent's Park Zoo in 1831, where the foreman reported that it did 'the work of six or eight men with scythes and brooms'. More importantly, he added that the surface left behind was a perfect one, with no marks on it.

Now, for the first time, it was possible for Everyman (or at least his servant) to mow the grass to make it into a lawn. But this was not the first mower, nor was it the first lawn. It was just the time when 'lawn' and 'mow' came together in collaboration, and they met with modified meanings.

Run a web search on 'Shakespeare on the lawn' as a phrase, and you will find around 4000 distinct hits covering performance programs in a number of countries where the plays are performed out of doors. These are lawns as we understand them today, but when Shakespeare set a scene on a lawn, he meant a different sort of lawn. *Macbeth*, act 3, scene 3 is set as follows: 'The same. A Park or Lawn, with a gate leading to the palace'.

Similarly, when Shakespeare set act 1, scene 2 of *As You Like It* on a 'Lawn before the Duke's palace', this was just an open space, clear of trees. Back then, a park or lawn was typically something that went in conjunction with a palace, and with being a king or some other Important Person.

A medieval lawn was more like a glade or grassy opening in a forest than the sort of lawn we know today. The famed medieval scholar, Albertus Magnus (1193–1280), studied plants. He distinguished the monocotyledons (a group that includes grasses and lilies) from the dicotyledons, the flowering plants with the showy flowers. But grasses are also flowering plants and Albertus knew this. He even wrote about the flowers' structures and was aware of 'our sort' of lawn, '... the sight is in no way so pleasantly refreshed as by fine and close grass kept short', he wrote.

Monasteries often had lawns in courtyards, and this is probably what Albertus had in mind. By Elizabethan times though, lawns were places where the upper classes took their leisure. Of course, Shakespeare also knew of lawn that was not made of grasses. In *Othello*, act 4, scene 3, when Shakespeare has Emilia speak of 'measures of lawn', we may need the words that follow ('gowns, petticoats … caps') if we are to understand her. The "lawn" Emilia refers to is linen fabric, fine thin cambric bleached on a lawn (meaning an open area between trees), instead of the ordinary bleaching grounds. While it is now more often made from cotton, this sort of lawn is still used for blouses, baby clothes, bishops' sleeves, ladies' handkerchiefs and the like.

Just as lawn was nothing new in 1830, so mowing was well understood. Notice how Budding suggested that his machine could replace the scythe. Human mowers, meaning men with scythes, were even then becoming machines that cut crops like barley and hay. One of the problems with researching the nineteenth century history of lawn mowers lies in distinguishing the mechanical mowers of agriculture which took in a crop, from the mechanical mowers designed to produce a nice velvety lawn, finished, polished and ready for people to use at and for their leisure.

Over time, the agricultural sense of mowing has faded from our consciousness. Just as most urban kids have little idea of where eggs or meat come from, so most of us have forgotten how farm animals must be fed in winter in cold climates. As we will see, our lawns and the mowing of them are the last vestigial link to agriculture for many. All the rest is a mystery.

In summer, many rural fields are mysteriously dotted with cylinders of hay, some plastic-wrapped. These sit on the stubble, waiting to be stored or sold. Unless we get the timing just right, we rarely witness the actual mowing as we flash past on the highway. Those cylinders might as well have been lowered from UFOs in the dead of night. The agricultural mower that reaps hay is hidden, and we only see and hear the domestic mower, because in the western world, lawn, as mown grass, is ubiquitous. Curiously, most lawn enthusiasts think that lawns are found only inside *their* national borders.

NATIONALIST LAWNS

Americans tend to care mightily about their lawns. If you ask a travelled American, you may get a grudging concession that one or two other English-speaking nations may share a hint of a profoundly limited and watered-down enthusiasm for lawn in a few places, for short periods, maybe. But most Americans usually assert that lawn is a purely American phenomenon.

Nobody wants to downgrade their own nation's lawn pre-eminence, but few citizens put their lawns on public display as Americans do. Many Australians have front lawns, but few Americans visit Australian suburbs to see them. Foreign tourists in America rush to see parks, buildings, bridges, statues, waterfalls, landscapes, canyons and the like, and foreign tourists in Australia target the deserts, the rainforests and the coral reefs. Suburbs just fail to draw crowds, and so the error in perception is compounded.

This same "only us" opinion can be heard from untravelled Australians and Britons as well. Foreigners, they will tell you, have no care for lawns, though film and television may have shown them something of the American love affair with grass. The better-informed Anglophones may generalise and say that lawn is an English-speaking thing. In fact, people have been saying it for some time. In 1875, the magazine *Living Age* found fault with Germany:

❝ We have seen that there is nothing in a German home (the flat being flattest) to particularly engage the loving care of its inmates. If you have swept, you need not

be guilty of the futile folly of garnishing your house also. You have no garden to cultivate, no greenhouse to potter round, no croquet-lawn to coddle, no window-flowers to encourage, no patent mower or beneficent hose to experimentalize with; the names of the commonest plants are unknown to German ladies, to whom talk of lobelias and petunias, calceolarias and verbenas, would be but babbling. 99

The poor quality of foreign lawns was a popular theme. Another *Living Age* article written in 1897 by C.J. Cornish (originally printed in *The Contemporary Review*), described outdoor life in Holland, and was rather scathing about Dutch lawns:

66 There is an English belief that 'Dutch gardening' is something very quaint, formal, and precise. The belief must date from an earlier period of Dutch history. Even those two great adjuncts of garden neatness, the roller and lawn mower, are almost unknown in Holland. The gardeners live under the belief that the way to make a lawn is to cut it as seldom as possible, and never to walk on it. As the subsoil is usually loose peaty sand, the grass is always thin, and the edges ragged. 99

These days, we can test the truth of such claims without a passport. Recall my view that it takes 50 years for the true social effects of a new technology to emerge, but that after 30 years, the effects begin to become apparent. As a case study in progress, take two modern offshoots of the 1969 internet, Google Earth and Google Maps street view. These may well be seen in the future as interesting change-makers, because they make armchair travellers of us all. Simple applications like that may expand our horizons without killing the planet with the massive carbon cost of jetting around.

While I have been germinating this book over the past two years, I have visited northern and western Australia, Vanuatu, Laos, Cambodia and Thailand, Greece, Cornwall and southern England, five states across the USA, Latvia, Lithuania and Estonia, Germany, Austria, the Netherlands and Belgium. I saw, observed and in most cases, sought out, lawn in each of those places. I was responsible for adding quite a few tons of carbon dioxide to the atmosphere, some of which was no doubt taken up by grass.

Thanks to my travels, I know that Brussels airport is surrounded by large houses with spacious backyards with trim green surfaces that must be lawn, but the two Google products make it easy for anybody to examine any suburb anywhere from the air and in some places, from street level. They can do it without any significant carbon cost from flying, and the Google Maps street view even allows us to judge, for ever-increasing parts of the globe, whether the lawns we see on our screen need mowing or not.

If travel broadens the mind, viewing satellite and other images on the internet is a passable cerebrum-widening tool which makes it fairly clear that while only a few nations care about front lawns as an adornment, many nations love their grass—and if the British did not start the trend, they certainly contributed to its spread.

If Americans *believe* they invented the lawn, Britons *know* they got there first. This explains a popular British gardening joke, where an American tourist goes up to a gardener at a Stately Home, and asks how they keep the lawn looking so green and lush. The gardener replies, 'Just water and roll every day, sir—for 500 years'. Australians probably console themselves that if they didn't think of lawns first, they care more about them.

The lawns seen in English formal gardens and in British university quadrangles had been admired and copied in America well before the first settlers reached Australia in 1788. There is a lawn in front of the state house in Dover, the capital of Delaware and according to the records, it was laid out in 1717 by a special commission of the Delaware General Assembly.

It is a beautifully proportioned lawn which sets off the elegant brick building. It speaks volumes for the hopes of the early colonists about creating a new England in a New World, and there are other lawns which existed before the colonies were transformed into some more or less united states in 1776. However you look at it, the British and the Americans were engaged with lawn quite a long while back.

�֎ ✸ ✸

THE ORIGINS OF THE MODERN LAWN

✠ ✠ ✠

A people without history is like wind on the buffalo grass.

— Sioux proverb.

Lawn is not just an Anglophone obsession or even just a western obsession, though the lawns of many other nations are public, not private. Lawn is a general human concern, though most nations care more about grass as a public or playing space. Some nations exalt lawn as a personal statement. For much of the western world, it isn't a home if there is no grass, or lawn, somewhere about the place.

There is a picture that circulates on the internet. It shows a US soldier in Iraq, tending a small plot of grass outside his tent in the desert. The accompanying story tells how his wife sent him the supplies. It all seems too good to be true, but apparently it is indeed true. The curious folk at the investigative website, www.snopes.com identified both the warrant officer who tended the plot and also the sergeant who took the picture. The aim (and in this case, it was mission accomplished!) was to deliver the aroma of grass and the feel of grass beneath the feet in a hostile zone.

The sturdy enquirers also turned up other cases of desert grass, including one piece located alongside a tent at Al Udeid Air Base in Doha, Qatar. It was reportedly the only grass on the base, but soldiers who rotated through the tent happily adopted and cared for it, watering it, trimming it with scissors, and rigging an awning to keep off the worst of the day's heat.

Now think of the European crusaders who invaded the Middle East in medieval times. They would not have cared about manicured lawn, because it was not part of their culture. Back at home, no lady, fretting in her castle,

cared whether or not her lord had a bit of lawn to look after or who would cut it if he failed to reappear. The sort of lawn that needed care was an alien concept, just a few hundred years ago.

Our sort of lawn is a recent development. Only modern humans have the time, the energy, the tools and the space to make a lawn out of some random wilderness, and perhaps only we crave the safety and security of having a lawn of our own.

Only the citizens of an industrial era could have deified the lawn. The wish to turn grass into lawn emerged when we began to take dominating nature for granted. We dared wish it because we were no longer quite so subject to nature's vagaries and whims. The lawn represents the meadows or pastures of earlier times and so it has to be grass. Our ancestors had grazing areas in yards, small plots, paddocks, fields and enclosures, but the ideal today is a space with a coating of trim lawn. Only real farmers may have real crops to admire, but urban people flaunt their lawns.

Having a lawn may be partly about security, but it is mainly about control and dominance. The lawn owner can claim to be monarch of all he surveys—and the gender assignment in this sentence was not made unthinkingly. Lawn care is very much a boy thing, even today, part of a desire to lord it over nature. Lawn is subservient, grass is subversive, grass is the anarchist vegetation that was celebrated by Malvina Reynolds in the 1960s:

**" God bless the grass
That grows through the crack.
They roll the concrete over it
To try and keep it back.
The concrete gets tired
Of what it has to do,
It breaks and it buckles,
And the grass grows through.
God bless the grass. "**

Reynolds' patient and persistent grass is a metaphor for freedom, for truth, for liberty. Grass is the human spirit that broke down the Berlin Wall, lawn represents the toiling huddled masses, groaning and suffering under the whip of an oppressor. It is no wonder that Michael Pollan described a lawn as 'nature under totalitarian rule'.

Lawn is a fertile place for amateur psychologists to play—and why not, when you consider the curious nature of the lawn fetish? Lawn owners prowl their lawns like bull sea elephants guarding their harem. I have even seen lawn maintenance likened to the sex act, but that is probably going just a bit too far. If we have to get analytical, I prefer Thorstein Veblen's take on lawn, even if it was delivered more than a century ago, when many aspects of the modern lawn fixation had not developed.

Veblen was the social critic and economist who coined the phrase 'conspicuous consumption'. In 1899, he wrote in *The Theory of the Leisure Class* that the 'lawn, or the close-cropped yard or park' appealed greatly to the taste of the Western peoples (read that as 'white'). He went further, and attributed the greatest love of lawn to the dolicho-blond (you can safely translate this as 'Aryan' for all working purposes) element in the population:

**" The lawn unquestionably has an element of
sensuous beauty ... no doubt it appeals pretty directly
to the eye of nearly all races and all classes; but it is,
perhaps, more unquestionably beautiful to the eye of
the dolicho-blond than to most other varieties of men.
This higher appreciation of a stretch of greensward in**

this ethnic element than in the other elements of the population, goes along with certain other features of the dolicho-blond temperament that indicate that this racial element had once been for a long time a pastoral people inhabiting a region with a humid climate. The close-cropped lawn is beautiful in the eyes of a people whose inherited bent it is to readily find pleasure in contemplating a well-preserved pasture or grazing land. 99

According to Veblen, the aesthetic purpose of the lawn is as a make-believe cow pasture. He argued that so long as the keeping of a cow will not be mistaken for thrift, a cow 'commonly of an expensive breed' may be kept on the lawn. That might have been feasible in 1899, but just imagine trying to get that past the enforcers of city or municipal ordinances today!

Veblen added that there was another side to the issue. If the luxurious surroundings did not make it clear that the cow was only for show, then 'the use of the cow as an object of taste must be avoided'. The home-owner should opt instead for some exotic (if less picturesque and pastoral) animal which would, by its cost or futility as an investment, show that it was by no means 'vulgarly lucrative either in fact or in suggestion'.

THE COST OF LAWN

Perhaps this explains why we spend so much on lawn mowers, leaf blowers and lawn decorations. The statistics vary, but estimates for North American lawns say there are between 20 and 32 million acres (about 8 to 13 million hectares) of lawn, with the lower end often being qualified as 'residential lawn'. All of this must be cared for and shown off, complete with accessories.

The statistics quoters all agree that this is more than the area devoted to any farm crop. Lawn owners spend an estimated US$750 million on grass seed alone. The total cost of caring for residential lawns in the USA is variously given as US$25 billion, or possibly US$30 billion or even US$40 billion. As we all know, 78.37% of all statistics are made up on the fly, so the minor discrepancies should only amaze us because they are so minor.

However you look, the US expenditure is an obscene amount. More than half the world's nations have a GDP of less that US$25 billion! Imagine what would happen if this area of lawn could be turned over to useful crops, or if that money could be devoted to aiding the Third World.

The lawn mowers and other ostentatious pieces of lawn equipment are just the modern equivalents of the antelope, the nineteenth century alpaca, or some other completely useless but living lawn pet. Today, alpacas are commercially useful, and so would be barred from being lawn pets. Appropriately, the lawn care machines are only vulgarly lucrative to those selling and servicing them. According to Veblen, public parks are a form of lawn, imitations of the pasture.

> " Such a park is of course best kept by grazing, and the cattle on the grass are themselves no mean addition to the beauty of the thing, as need scarcely be insisted on with anyone who has once seen a well-kept pasture. But it is worth noting, as an expression of the pecuniary element in popular taste, that such a method of keeping public grounds is seldom resorted to. "

This was 1899, and in the USA. Cattle had been removed from British parks by then, even if sheep were still sometimes present. Cattle might have been more picturesque than sheep but the clear appearance of thrift and usefulness in running cattle on the grass ruled them out. To the solid citizen of the late nineteenth century, cattle on the public pleasure ground would seem intolerably cheap and offensively indecorous, and that was without considering the health risks, real or imagined.

The French admired their lawns as a part of the surroundings of a fine home, but even by 1757, Denis Diderot wrote in his Encyclopédie that the English were the kings of the lawn and, though the French tried to imitate them, 'lawns in France are not fine, nor treated, nor a beautiful green ... not rolled or mowed with the care and intelligence necessary ...'

When we consider lawn, we need to distinguish two separate types. There are public lawns on the large scale, and the private lawns belonging to residences, which their owners use to advertise their status. Wherever you go, from Louis XIV's palace at Versailles near Paris to the Thai king's royal palace at Ayutthaya to the White House and Windsor Castle, there are lawns. The hope behind these lawns is that worthy citizens will follow their leaders' lead, even if their lawn is no larger than a pocket handkerchief.

A quick flight over the world using the satellite system of your choice will reveal that there are lawns in or near homes in Copenhagen, Quito, Capetown, Singapore, Rio, Riga, Florence and New Zealand. All the world loves a lawn—if they can have one. Guards on bicycles chase tourists off the lawn at the Schönbrunn Palace in Vienna, blowing whistles at those with deficient German.

In September 1942, gardening writers in Britain had little creative stuff to write about because everybody was growing extra food. In a bid to lighten the gloom and lessen the load, The Times addressed the question of what a lawn should be. A garden lawn, its readers were told, was meant to act as a framework for beds, borders and single specimens. Clearly, that did not demand grass which in turn demanded care and affection. Instead, the gardener might use heather for a springy lawn. It was tolerant of being walked on, but wild thyme and 'Chamomile' would also do, added the writer.

A mere patch of grass is not a lawn, because it has not been sufficiently cultivated, cultured and venerated. We often speak interchangeably about turf, grass and lawn, and in most of the world, all three would be treated as cropped plantations of selected members of the grass family. On the other hand, some English gardeners can contemplate with equanimity the idea of a camomile lawn, a lawn of low-lying daisy plants.

In Japan, moss lawns are common, and other damp areas also tend to favour moss. The moss lawns may not be durable under heavy feet, but they are hardy enough, and they make a nice uniform velvet texture in bright green. Be kind to the cryptogams, because one day, they may inherit the earth—or at least your yard!

THE NATURE OF GRASS

If 'lawn' is loosely defined and open to interpretation, the same cannot be said of grass, turf and turfgrass. To botanists, the name 'grass' indicates a member of the Poaceae—or Gramineae, as they used to be called. The plants

THE lawn mower was the only choice for a well-kept lawn, though Marie Antoinette may have had other thoughts on that. In the late eighteenth century, before she met the guillotine, the ill-fated French queen had sheep as her playthings, pretty pastoral sheep with satin bows that she could walk along with, as she played at being a shepherdess. Unlike King George III, otherwise known as 'Farmer George', and his grandson-in-law, Prince Albert, there was no thought of turning a profit behind her activities.

in this family have certain characteristics in common; 'turf' is a cultivated patch of a grass (or grasses) which is mowed to produce a close cover of roots and stems; a 'turfgrass' is a species or cultivated variety of grass, generally with a spreading habit, that can be used to develop turf. On the other hand, any patch of low greenery on which the owner spends a small fortune probably qualifies (to the owner) as lawn.

Our whole human world revolves around grasses. Rice, wheat, rye, corn and millet are all grasses, so are the bamboos used in much of Asia as building materials for low dwellings, high scaffolding and rafts, but bamboo lawns will never happen. Much of our plant intake is made up of the seeds of grasses, and our meat comes mainly from animals that browse on grass. A world without grasses would be a very different world, and so would a world without lawn, but we would miss the grasses far more than we would ever rue the lack of lawn.

Then there is the hay phenomenon. Some historians argue that at some point in the Dark Ages, somebody in northern Europe had the idea of cutting the long grass in autumn and storing it to feed horses and cattle in the winter. Hay was unknown in ancient Rome, because at Rome's latitude, there is enough winter grass to keep animals alive. North of the Alps, the animals starved and died in winter. Once the idea of hay making became widely known in medieval Europe, there was nothing to stop northern tribes keeping oxen and horses to move goods and food, and even to provide power for simple machinery. Once they had access to hay, northern villages could swell to become cities, tribes could become nations and a new power balance arose, based on grass.

All flesh is grass, says the Bible, but all civilisation is grass as well, or at least grass-based. Grass is amazingly productive stuff if it is left to itself. All the same, First World nations prefer the non-productive grasses in lawns. The same effort would fill the hungry bellies of the world, if it were better managed, or it could fill many of their fuel tanks, just as grass was once used to fuel draught animals.

Now let us return to the names of grasses, because botany can be a bit anarchic when it comes to the naming of things. The anarchy is only partial, because at the lower levels, there are tight rules about how a species or a genus is named and renamed. Species names do not change too much, but at the genus level and higher, people are free to divide or re-divide a grouping, or to move species. That can sometimes mean that several names may be used for a single group or species, but over time, one name usually becomes adopted.

To a conservative older botanist, all grasses belong to a family called the Gramineae, a name given to them in the 1750s by Carl von Linné or Linnaeus. (He invented the 'Latin' naming system for plants and animals, so this may be why we often use the Latin form of his name as well.) These days, plant families all end in '-aceae', pronounced 'acey', with a few exceptions that are left over from the time of Linnaeus. Today, you will often find newer systems and younger botanists calling the grass family the Poaceae. It matters little, because most botanists are sufficiently agile to know both names, even if one or the other makes them 'harumph', slightly.

Whatever group you assign them to, a grass is a plant with a tubular jointed stem and sheathing leaf bases that arise from the joints and wrap around, often concealing the stem. Bamboos are grass stems on a grand scale, but pluck a grass runner from the ground, and you will see a similar plan to that of bamboo. Of course, the fact that grass has runners is part of the key to its success, because it spreads out, covering an area, and often choking out all other plant growth.

Thanks to the bamboos, you can even find grass forests. These are the bamboo forests of Asia, which are as close to monocultures as any lawn, subject to the variation that comes from wind and storm, and the depredations of the giant panda and the bamboo rat. The bamboos evade the grazing of most mammals by towering far above them, but other grasses have evolved to evade grazers by cowering below them, flat on the ground so their stems and roots stay intact, even as their leaves are cropped and eaten. These are the grasses that may make a lawn.

THE NATURE OF LAWN PLANTS

So what makes a lawn plant? Any vegetation that survives grazing or mowing that trims the plant almost to ground level can make a lawn, but survival isn't easy. Most flowering plants have a growing point near the tip of a shoot, and if these tips are repeatedly cut off, the plant responds first by producing many new branchlets, something that topiarists and hedge makers rely on. But if the tips are cut often enough, the plant will die.

The weeds that do best in a mown lawn are the rosette plants. These are species and varieties with a vastly shortened stem, so the growing tip stays close to the ground, below the reach of mower blades and incisor teeth. This shortness may help save the plant, but it puts it at risk of being dangerously overshadowed by grasses that can rise above it, so most rosette plants completely cover a patch of ground in order to safely lock out any competing grasses.

Grasses can climb above the weeds because they sprout differently. Even though the grasses can grow high if they are allowed to, they grow mainly from the crown, a small area where both the roots and the stems originate. Grasses have growth points at their joints as well, so when they encounter a mower, either a mechanical one or an animal's teeth, the buds at the joints can send out new runners, but if a straggly grass is rolled up and chomped short, the crown remains to send out new shoots.

The crown is even closer to the ground than the growing tip of a rosette plant, so the crown is an ideal recovery mechanism, unless you set the blades of your mower too low. That takes out the crown, causing 'scalping'. This is an apt name, because a scalped human can grow no hair, and scalped grass can send up no new shoots and leaves.

The best lawn grasses are the ones that spread by sending out runners, though these are technically divided into stolons that go above the ground and rhizomes that are underground. It matters little because each is a stem that spreads sideways and then puts down roots and sends up shoots, establishing what is effectively a new plant, covering the ground and improving the ability of the grass to choke out weeds that may seek to get in.

Perennial ryegrass has a name which tells us that it keeps growing, year after year, and we see it most commonly when we watch tennis at The Championships in Wimbledon, or the US Masters golf at the Augusta National Golf Club in Georgia. In each case, the perennial ryegrass that you see has been freshly planted for the year because long experience has shown that this works best for the sport in question.

Of course, the 10,000 or so species of grass had a great deal of time to specialise, even before the horticulturists started selecting and breeding them.

EVOLUTION AND GRASS

Depending on the evidence you accept, grasses may have emerged as a recognisable group around 55 million years ago, but recent evidence from India suggests that the grasses are even older. The 55 million year age is the youngest possible because there are fossils from then. These are very clearly grasses because they show outlines of easily visible leaves and stems, but searchers have found nothing earlier.

The real problem is that very few individual grasses ever end up as fossils, so botanists have no idea what the earliest grasses looked like. Maybe we will find fossils of the first grasses next week, but maybe we won't. All we can say is that by the time the known fossil record begins, the grasses had adapted and specialised. This is hardly surprising when you consider that most of the grasses were low, juicy and easy for browsing animals to reach.

A situation like that tends to provide a powerful selection effect, so the grasses that lived were the ones that had some sort of defence against being eaten, or the ones that produced the most seed, or seed that could be spread efficiently to new places.

Perhaps we have found no fossils before 55 million years ago because we have been looking in the wrong places. Vandana Prasad and colleagues found a clue in coprolites, fossil fecal pellets left behind by dinosaurs in the late Cretaceous period. These fossils were formed over 65 million years ago, not long before the dinosaurs disappeared, around the time when Gondwana broke apart.

Evolution is an arms race, where each improvement demands counter-improvements in other plants and animals. As a food plant or animal develops a new defence, only those predators able to cope with the defence are able to live and reproduce, but there are many ways of coping.

Australian gum trees (*Eucalyptus*) produce a toxic oil, sold around the world as antiseptic eucalyptus oil. Australian koalas eat the oil-filled leaves and cope with this poisonous mix by having a very small brain and sitting around all day—they need less energy, and so need to eat less, which saves them from being poisoned by the oils. Koalas may sit around looking cuddly: in reality, they are just clinging to life.

There are probably other mammals in Australia which stopped eating eucalyptus long ago because they couldn't cope with the toxins. If any animal species ever develops an enzyme that can destroy the poisons in the oil, it will have an incredible larder. Any gum tree that can then produce a different and unbreakable toxin will have a real advantage. So the struggle goes on.

All over the world, small fights like that are going on as plants produce poisons and browsers try to overcome them. Monarch caterpillars in North America even take up poisons called cardiac glycosides from milkweeds, and use these to make themselves taste unpleasant which stops blue jays eating them. Score one to the butterflies!

Grasses and some other plants have an effective defence against predators in the form of small nodules of silica. The smallest rock wallaby in Australia is the nabarlek (*Petrogale concinna*). The wallabies themselves are smaller members of the hopping marsupials group that includes kangaroos, but there is something more important about the nabarlek than its size. It is the only marsupial mammal which is able to replace its molar or grinding teeth, over and over again. This makes sense if you know that this tiny wallaby prefers to eat grasses rich in silica.

The small pieces of silica are sharp, so they cut the mouth, tongue and lips of any animal that tries to eat them, but silica is also a very hard mineral, which is why it rapidly wears away the teeth of grazers. If they are swallowed, the tiny and very distinctive silica pieces are not digested, but eventually pass out of the gut, unchanged. Without the ability to grow new molar teeth, the nabarlek would soon have no teeth, and so it would starve to death.

When these silica nodules are found in the environment, they are called phytoliths, which means 'plant stones'. They are tiny but recognisable, and if they show up in a late Cretaceous deposit, this suggests that there must have been grasses around in the late Cretaceous. They do indeed appear in those deposits, but more importantly, the phytoliths turn up in fossil dinosaur poo. So, say scientists, the dinosaurs must have eaten some grasses, which means the grasses are older than we thought.

The most popular theory to explain the way the dinosaurs disappeared involves an asteroid striking the Earth. There undoubtedly was an asteroid, but not everybody is convinced that it did away with the dinosaurs, because a number of scientists think some of the dinosaurs got around their problems by evolving into birds.

Flowering plants are one of the suspects for killing off the dinosaurs that died, and grasses are flowering plants. It is possible that just eating the grasses wiped out many of the herbivorous dinosaurs and perhaps wiped out the whole dinosaur ecology. That would have left the way open for new systems involving grasslands, horses, deer and cattle relatives, dung beetles and even some primates, our remote ancestors. Then again, grasses may have had nothing to do with it at all. We can only say for certain that grass-like phytoliths were swallowed by late Cretaceous dinosaurs in what is now India.

If it seems a little far-fetched to point the finger at grasses as the nemesis of the dinosaurs, consider the research carried out in 2008 on populations of voles (*Microtus agrestis*) living in Kielder Forest, in northern England. Voles are rodents, and these particular voles mainly eat tufted hairgrass (*Deschampsia caespitosa*) in winter.

Usually, when a population of animals goes through a boom–bust cycle, the driving force is the predator. In this case, that would appear to be the vole, but it is the grass that is actually in control. Studies over time have shown that when vole numbers are high, the silica deposits on the grass are also high, and when vole numbers are low, so are the silica levels. Voles seem to avoid high silica grass, which is probably good for them, since the high silica content makes them lose weight, probably by interfering with their digestion of proteins.

The researchers noted that there was probably an energy cost to the grasses in extracting the silicon from the soil and depositing it in the leaves, and this cost would make the grass less competitive against other grasses that the vole does not eat. Somehow, heavier grazing triggers the secretion of silica in the grass leaves. So you never know: perhaps other grasses may have had a similar effect on dinosaurs.

Back, though, to the origins of the grasses. The coprolites were found in central India, and they are associated with the bones of huge plant-eating dinosaurs called titanosaurs. More importantly, the phytoliths are of five kinds, suggesting that the titanosaurs were grazing on five different species

of grass, though analysis suggests that grasses were still only a small part of the total diet.

This sheds light on a parallel mystery. Some early mammals called the gondwanatherians lived alongside the dinosaurs. These mammals had high-crowned teeth, more suitable for eating grasses than other plants, but until the coprolite find, palaeontologists assumed there were no grasses alive then. Now, based on the dinosaur coprolites, we believe that grasses *were* around, and that the wide-mouthed gondwanatherians and the titanosaurs may already have been 'mowing' the grass.

Perhaps the dinosaurs started the whole process of selecting those species that were most likely to lie low under grazing and make a good lawn. Those of us who can trace our ancestry back to the pre-lawn days when the Normans invaded England tend to feel rather pleased with ourselves, but the lawn itself may be able to trace its way right back to the dinosaurs!

In the middle of the nineteenth century, biologists took on board Darwin's notion that all life forms had arisen because of the interactions between variations of different species. That was also the time when gardeners began to treasure rare and unusual plants from exotic places like the Amazon or Yunnan, yet their lawns were becoming monocultures. To anybody with even an inkling of ecological understanding, with even a minuscule insight into what Darwin was saying, creating a monoculture lawn is crazy. Today, people are beginning to see this. An American friend, knowing I was working on this book, emailed me:

> " I believe in Darwinian gardening, so my lawn contains the hardier grasses, dandelions, violets, and even bugleweed and patches of moss. "

The notion of a Darwinian lawn seems to arise often. I must confess that when I was a lawn owner, several of my smaller patches of lawn suffered regular additions of new species. Spencer Herbert came up with the notion of 'survival of the fittest' after reading Darwin, but I still hoped for an indirectly Darwinian lawn. It was not quite a fair test, because I used to discourage the kikuyu grass by pulling out any long runners, opening gaps for the other species. So? I was just another picky browser on the lawn!

Then again, I have the ecologist's innate distrust of monocultures lurking in my mind. Big agriculture faces the risk every day that a pest will get into a crop, and then behave like a child in a sweet shop. Broad plains of wheat, giant paddies of rice and pristine forests of pine all face the same risk of a massive invasion by a pest. Big Agriculture copes by massive applications of chemicals that we hope are selectively toxic. This hope is rarely met, and the same applies when Big Lawn is maintained in the same way.

The complexities of the American prairie or the English field with its hedgerows were being reduced, driven to a dull uniformity. There was a patina, an imitation of variability there, because the lawn offered an attractive hunting ground to birds that fed on seeds and insects that could find no cover on or under the grass. Lawns which attracted birds just had to be rich, thought the lawn owners as they added birdbaths and other items to bring yet more birds.

Mammals, reptiles, amphibians, insects and leaf litter invertebrates all lost out because they could find neither food nor cover, and in time, even the birds found that they were on a lush green desert, as devoid of food for them as it was for the birds that were nectar sippers. Even the grasses found the lawn devoid of food, because clovers that might have provided nitrates to the soil were ruthlessly destroyed. Now nitrate has to be provided from a bag instead.

MEANS, MOTIVE AND OPPOTRUNITY COME TOGETHER

✳ ✳ ✳

Humans have been farming for some 10,000 years, long enough for some farming instincts to have evolved in many of us. Some radical educators even divide boys into 'hunters' and 'farmers'. On this theory, the hunters were the ones who went out into the wilderness, generation after generation, and often died, far from home. They were the adventurers, the explorers, the dreamers and the soldiers. The farmers, the boys and men who were inclined to stay at home, were the ones who settled and were satisfied with their lot, their plot, their field of crops.

In our industrial age, more of the farmer-type men have lost their close connection with the soil, but they have found a handy substitute in their lawns. The hunters were still around, but they found less opportunity for wild deeds in the wilderness as they also became locked into work. By an odd chance, they also found satisfaction on grass, as new team sports were invented, games played on fields of grass that were made playable by the wielding of the lawn mower. Hunters are generally better at sports than farmers.

Farmers and hunters alike, men and boys are subject to peer pressure. The idea of making lawn affected both as the toiling men rendered their lawns sterile and uniform. The suburban farmers were driven by inner forces, but even the suburban hunters found themselves constrained to maintain neatness and order on what was, in several senses, their home turf.

There was another aspect, the hygiene imperative. In many ways, this was based on a wrong model, a view of disease as something caused by bad smells and untidiness. On this theory, surfaces must be cleaned, dusted and painted, bad smells had to be eliminated, and tidiness was next to godliness. It was a flawed model, but it worked to an extent, because doing away with the unsightly often managed to clear away sources of infection that might otherwise lurk around the home.

In January 1820, a report appeared in *The Times*, which puts a different slant on the mowing imperative. In the previous year, in Sierra Leone between 1 June and 24 August, more than 50 of about 120 people

(presumably British) had died of disease. The informant added that his street was covered with ling grass and high weeds which were accused of taking up the moisture of the unguttered street and emitting putrid effluvia. This, said the informant, was a nuisance which might have been avoided by employing African prisoners to cut them down.

> **"** ... when the swamp grasses, weeds, sedges, and various plants in which mosquitoes find refuge after transformation are cut down and cleared away,—when, in short, the scythe, lawn-mower, grubbing-axe, and gardener's hand of diligence, thrift, cleanliness, and care have turned our country into a cultivated garden, the days of the mosquito as a pest will be numbered. **"**

Cleanliness and sweet smells were all one needed to defeat disease in the days when Australian eucalyptus trees were planted all over the world to help in the fight against malaria. The fight was thought to be effectively taken to malaria with the sweet-smelling oils that came from their leaves. In 1857, *Scientific American* revealed how the plants were believed to have helped defeat disease in Washington DC, even at the horrible cost of harming a lawn. The 'ague' referred to is better known to us these days as malaria.

" *Sun Flowers a preventive of Fever and Ague.*

Whether the sun flowers planted in a miasmatic situation will prevent persons who reside in the neighborhood from being affected with fever and ague or not, we personally cannot tell, but others who have tried the experiment have asserted 'they will.' Lieut. Maury, of Washington, through the columns of the *Rural New Yorker*, has given his views on the subject. He states that he made an experiment last year with the cultivation of sun flowers as a preventive or protection against ague and fever.

At the risk of spoiling a beautiful lawn, he made the gardener trench up to the depth of two a half feet a belt about forty-five feet broad around the Observatory on the marshy side, and from 150 to 200 yards from the buildings. After being well manured from the stable yard, the ground was properly prepared and planted in sun flowers in the spring of 1836. They grew finely. The sickly season was expected with more than the usual anxiety.

Finally it set in, and there was shaking at the President's House and other places, as usual, but for the first time since the Observatory was built the watchmen about it weathered the summer clear of chills and fevers. These men, being most exposed to the night air, suffer most, and heretofore two or three relays of them would be attacked during the season; for, as one falls sick, another is employed in his place, who, in turn, being attacked, would in like manner give way to a fresh hand. "

Today, we'd suspect that the trench served to drain the marsh, reducing mosquito breeding places, but that sort of insight was in the future. As long as false inferences brought results, cleanliness remained next to godliness.

Long after the invention of the lawn mower, scythes had their place in maintaining hygiene and tidiness. In Australia, long grass was seen as a potential haven for snakes and as fuel for bushfires so grass still needed to be mowed. Ethel Turner published her children's classic, *Seven Little Australians*, in 1894, and in this, we read of Judy (or Helen, to her father), the doomed young heroine, applying a scythe:

" Outside in the blazing sunshine Judy was mowing the lawn.

They only kept one man, and, as his time was so taken up with the horses and stable work generally, the garden was allowed to fall into neglect. More than once the Captain had spoken vexedly of the untidy lawns, and said he was ashamed for visitors to come to the house. So Judy, brimming over with zeal, armed herself with an abnormally large scythe, and set to work on the long, long grass.

'Good heavens, Helen! you'll cut your legs off!' called her father, in an agitated tone.

He had stepped out on to the front veranda for a mild cigar after the mulberry just as she brought her scythe round with an admirable sweep and decapitated a whole army of yellow-helmeted dandelions.

She turned and gave him a beautiful smile. 'Oh, no, Father!—why, I'm quite a dab at mowing.'

She gave it another alarming but truly scientific sweep. 'See that—and th-a-at—and tha-a-a-at!'

'Th-a-at' carried off a fragment of her dress, and 'tha-a-a-at' switched off the top of a rose-bush; but there are details to everything, of course.

'Accidents will happen, even to the best regulated grass-cutters,' she said composedly, and raising the scythe for a fresh circle. "

Judy's father, Captain Woolcot, is alarmed that he will need to 'provide you with cork legs and re-stock the garden', but Judy perseveres. Later, when she dies, as heroines often did in those times, Turner milks the pathos as hard as she can in this description of her bereaved father's reaction:

66 The Captain never smoked at the end of the side veranda now: the ill-kept lawn made him see always a little figure in a pink frock and battered hat mowing the grass in a blaze of sunlight. Judy's death made his six living children dearer to his heart, though he showed his affection very little more. **99**

THE PERILS OF HYGIENE

The hygiene fetish can go too far, of course. There is a curious effect known among asthma specialists. It is a correlation, and it is important to remember that correlations between A and B do not imply that A causes B, any more than they imply that B causes A. In this case, the correlation is between the number of McDonalds outlets in a particular country, and the per capita incidence of asthma.

Fast food does not cause asthma, but there may be an indirect link. More affluent countries are usually those where people have caught the hyper-hygiene bug. In those places, infants may not get a sufficient level of exposure to germs, and this may deleteriously affect their immune systems and somehow cause asthma, later on. Those same affluent countries are more able to afford fast food, hence the increased business for assorted burger chains and the 'link'.

Those same countries usually also love their lawns. So far, nobody seems to have calculated the correlation between per capita lawn acreage and asthma incidence, but once again, an effect ought to show up, because a nation that loves its lawns is a nation that detests, loathes and fears germs. At first glance, lawn does not cause asthma either, though grass pollens could well be implicated. There are also apparent links between excessive hygiene and Type I diabetes, and grass cannot be blamed there!

We need a little bit of dirt, a modicum of wilderness, a tad of untidiness in our lives. If your lawn is the sort that makes neighbourly noses twitch, slip that argument into the conversation, and remember Jay Gatsby's fate. F. Scott Fitzgerald may have implied through Nick that it was a jealous husband, but I am inclined to think it was lawn rage on Nick's part.

" 'I want to get the grass cut,' he said.

We both looked at the grass—there was a sharp line where my ragged lawn ended and the darker, well-kept expanse of his began. I suspected that he meant my grass. **"**

F. Scott Fitzgerald, *The Great Gatsby*, chapter 5.

SUBURBS, LAWNS AND CASTES

" Oak Park is a neighborhood of wide lawns and narrow minds. **"**

Ernest Hemingway, supposedly describing the town where he was born, source unconfirmed.

In 1868, Frederick Law Olmsted laid out the new suburban precinct of Riverside in Chicago. Breaking with tradition, he did away with fences at the front, though most urban properties then were built on the street alignment and needed no fences. City homes had no visible grass, no garden, no hint of green out front, even if they had a yard at the back. Olmsted changed this pattern when he set his houses thirty feet back from the property line, providing majestic front lawns for the residents. The effect was of one continuous park, with houses in a line along it, and a special park, where each of the house owners also owned, and took responsibility for, a small slice.

In the middle of the nineteenth century, goats were common on Australian city streets and pigs were common enough in American cities. Both species were expected to contribute to local garbage disposal. Hens were common, even in cities, as were cattle, because in the days before pasteurisation and refrigeration, milk needed to be taken from the cow and sold fast before it went off. All in all, people needed fences to keep their stock in, and others' stock out.

IN cities around the world, the 1860s saw new public transport as horse omnibuses and horse trams were replaced with steam and then electric light rail (streetcars, trolley-cars or trams). These brought the suburbs within reach of the towns, so that industrialists and even workers could move away from the factories and their fumes. At first, only the rich could afford a lawn. Soon, though, the idea of lawn would percolate down.

As populations grew and cities became more squalid, animals were banished and fences became unnecessary, but it was a slow change.

Tradition blames Mrs O'Leary's cow for the next step. After an 1871 fire left 100,000 people in Chicago homeless, timber buildings were banished to the edge of town, with steel and stone 'skyscrapers' in the centre. The cow was probably innocent of kicking over a lamp to start the blaze, but the fire, whatever its cause, moved a whole lot of people out of the city in a hurry, swelling the suburbs even faster.

The cities expanded and in time, even trams and streetcars could not carry enough people fast enough. Starting with London as far back as the 1850s, underground railways like London's Tube, systems called the Metro in many cities and even a few elevated railroads, shifted people to and from work. More importantly, they delivered workers home in time for men to tend their lawns. Through the 1870s and the 1880s, the world's cities acquired fast steam-powered transport to carry people home to their suburbs, and suburban culture flourished.

THE RISE OF THE PUBLIC PARK

We will come back to those matters in a while: first we need to visit the tradition of landscaping in Britain and see how it became transferred to public parks in the nineteenth century, all over the world, because parks were Olmsted's inspiration at Riverside. Something happened in the mid-nineteenth century to make city parks an attractive idea. Existing parks changed in their form, but many new parks were constructed with pleasant paths, planned plantings and exceedingly well-kept lawns where one might saunter.

It must surely have been some sort of reaction to the visible and horrifying effects of the slums in the industrial world, but it seems to have happened in a number of places. This came home to me when I was wandering through Amsterdam's Vondelpark, and read in the guidebook that it was 'a typical park of the 1860s'. The architect, L.D. Zocher was told to design it as 'an English landscape'. The Vondelpark is still there, somewhat battered under the pounding of feet as pedestrians walk over the grass to avoid the inline skaters, the cyclists and the homeless, but everybody seems to get along.

Like the Vondelpark, today's parks are democratic and free, but there was a time, when parks were very much the preserve of the rich, when fences around the outside of an estate grandly named as a park might warn of 'gins and steel traps' within. These were devices held ready to trap wily poaching trespassers. In chapter 6 of *Mansfield Park*, Jane Austen reflects an enthusiasm for 'improvement' that was common from the late eighteenth century onwards. It was a time for landscape gurus, usually clever gardeners, to seek their own improvement, at the expense of those who had made their pile.

The family which owned Mansfield Park was rich because they owned sugar plantations in the West Indies, worked by slave labour. Such families were *nouveau riche* types, and while impoverished aristocrats might allow the sugar millionaires to marry their younger offspring, those who had become suddenly rich from the juice of that giant grass, sugar cane, were regarded as appropriate targets for the witty pens of novelists.

The property's name is a sly reference to Lord Mansfield, a judge who is famous for saying 'the air of England is too pure for a slave to breathe', even though he never said it! A similar comment was quoted by counsel representing James Somersett, the slave who was freed by Mansfield in 'Somersett's Case' in 1772, but tradition has put the words in the judge's mouth. So with that warning, read Austen's skewering of the rich and tasteless:

> **" [Mr Rushworth] had been visiting a friend in the neighbouring county, and that friend having recently had his grounds laid out by an improver, Mr Rushworth was returned with his head full of the subject, and very eager to be improving his own place in the same way; and though not saying much to the purpose, could talk of nothing else. The subject had been already handled in the drawing-room; it was revived in the dining-parlour. Miss Bertram's attention and opinion was evidently his chief aim; and though her deportment showed rather conscious superiority than any solicitude to oblige him, the mention of Sotherton Court, and the ideas attached to it, gave her a feeling of complacency, which prevented her from being very ungracious.**

'I wish you could see Compton,' said he; 'it is the most complete thing! I never saw a place so altered in my life. I told Smith I did not know where I was. The approach now, is one of the finest things in the country: you see the house in the most surprising manner. I declare, when I got back to Sotherton yesterday, it looked like a prison ...'

'Oh, for shame!' cried Mrs Norris. 'A prison indeed? Sotherton Court is the noblest old place in the world.'

'It wants improvement, ma'am, beyond anything. I never saw a place that wanted so much improvement in my life; and it is so forlorn that I do not know what can be done with it.'

'No wonder that Mr Rushworth should think so at present,' said Mrs Grant to Mrs Norris, with a smile; 'but depend upon it, Sotherton will have every improvement in time which his heart can desire.'

'I must try to do something with it,' said Mr Rushworth, 'but I do not know what. I hope I shall have some good friend to help me.'

'Your best friend upon such an occasion,' said Miss Bertram calmly, 'would be Mr Repton, I imagine.'

'That is what I was thinking of. As he has done so well by Smith, I think I had better have him at once. His terms are five guineas a day.'

'Well, and if they were ten,' cried Mrs Norris, 'I am sure you need not regard it. The expense need not be any impediment. If I were you ... I would have everything done in the best style, and made as nice as possible. Such a place as Sotherton Court deserves everything that taste and money can do.' **99**

Those who had money could buy taste, but they wanted value for money. Like managers today, they set great store by what they could measure, such as the smoothness of lawns—never mind the subsoil. There would be no rubs on their lawns, or they would know the reason why!

THE LAWN AS PLAYING SURFACE

Even those who can muddle on for a few lines past Hamlet's introductory 'To be, or not to be', soon fall by the wayside, but as the soliloquy approaches the half-way point there comes a familiar phrase that may help them stagger on for a line or two. 'Ay, there's the rub', says Hamlet.

Many generations of school children have been subjected to the play, read aloud in a classroom. This is invariably accompanied by a withering fusillade of sterile literary criticism, an experience devoid of charm, wit or joy. Still, those children all learn that 'rub' comes from the sport of lawn bowls. The rub was a spot, a flaw, a rough patch on the lawn that deflected the ball from its path, derailing the intended effect.

I know what a rub is, because I 'learned' English literature that way. I recall wondering what the playwright meant, being well familiar with the billiard-table surfaces of local bowling greens, places where, if a carelessly kicked football fell on the green during a game, elders would shout with rage and hurl it back at us along with slights about our parentage and the vile deeds that must have been achieved to generate us and our parents before us.

If they were absent, we knew enough to save the grassy surface by taking off our shoes and stepping gently. Sir Francis Drake supposedly played lawn bowls before going out to defeat the Armada, and he would have known all about the rub—a term which first came into use about that time—because Drake almost certainly played the game on a camomile lawn, a rough and variable surface composed of daisy plants.

The English lawn had its beginnings in Tudor times, but it was far less likely to be grass. At some point around the eighteenth century, sheep beyond the 'ha-ha' helped make a new style of lawn. The ha-ha kept sheep, cows, goats, donkeys, horses (or their by-products) from appearing too close to the house. It was a wall, fence or hedge, placed in a ditch.

From the Big House, the ha-ha was an invisible barrier to the animals cropping the outer grass, while men with scythes did the same thing, closer-in. Between them, the distant animals beyond the ha-ha and the nearby men inside it delivered the idealised lawn. At his Mount Vernon home, George Washington employed English gardeners. His inner lawn was mown by hand and beyond the ha-ha, browsing deer kept the rest tidy.

FROM PRIVATE PARKS TO PUBLIC PARKS

In 1764, Capability Brown was appointed Master Gardener at Hampton Court. At the same time, George III engaged Brown to re-landscape Richmond Gardens, where he favoured gently undulating lawns and water views seen between trees. This set a pattern for the aristocracy and rich commoners in England, for the genteel citizens of the colonies and also for the improvers and landscapers who came on the scene in the steps of Capability Brown.

Among them was Joseph Paxton. He was working in the Chiswick Gardens on land owned by the immensely rich William Spencer Cavendish, the 6th Duke of Devonshire when they met. The duke hired him to take charge of his own rather neglected gardens, next door at Chatsworth, which gave him his start. Here is the story of his first day there:

> " I left London by the Comet coach for Chesterfield, arrived at ... half past four o'clock in the morning of the ninth of May, 1826. As no person was to be seen at that early hour, I got over the greenhouse gate by the old covered way, explored the pleasure-grounds, and looked around the outside of the house. I then went down to the kitchen-gardens, scaled the outside wall, and saw the whole of the place, set the men to work there at six o'clock; then returned to Chatsworth and got Thomas Weldon to play me the water-works, and afterwards, went to breakfast with poor dear Mrs Gregory and her niece (Sarah Brown); the latter fell in love with me, and I with her, and thus completed my first morning's work ... before nine o'clock. "

Paxton was clearly a man who did not let the grass grow beneath his feet. He was not an educated man, and there is a legend, probably true, that Queen Victoria was amused when Paxton addressed her on the subject of the 'hextinct hanimals' near the Crystal Palace. That morning, Paxton was only 23, just a labourer's son with ambition but no formal education, who died as Sir Joseph Paxton MP, a famous man who left an estate valued at some US$20 million in today's terms.

He married his Sarah Brown who became his business partner and administrator, as well as bearing him six children. He also developed hothouses where bananas, dahlias, and orchids could grow in a cold climate. These inspired the designs for the Crystal Palace buildings in London and New York, though that came later. Before then, he moved on to bigger landscape tasks. One was the first publicly funded park in Britain. This was Birkenhead Park, which was to become the practical start of a trend that reached around the world.

Until 1820, Birkenhead was an isolated agricultural area, close to teeming, stinking industrial Liverpool, but on the other side of the river. In that year, a steam ferry across the Mersey River made it accessible to Liverpool, both as a residential area and as an industrial area. The population began to grow fast, but in the early 1830s, people were becoming aware of the problems that beset all new industrial sites.

One result of this concern was something called the 'Parks Movement', a group which argued that open spaces for public use were good for workers. In 1841, a scheme for a public park at Birkenhead was proposed, and in 1843, the Birkenhead Commissioners bought land on which to establish the world's first publicly-funded park. The allocated ground was 185 acres in size but no bargain, a mean low-lying plot of marsh and common, a place of illegal gambling and dog fighting.

Of this land, 125 acres were set aside for the park; the remainder was to be sold to fund the construction work, and also Paxton's fee of £800. Major plantings took place in 1844–45, work was almost complete in 1846, and the opening took place in 1847. It was a remarkable success, and in spring, 1850, an American named Frederick Law Olmsted (he who would design Chicago's Riverside) came to visit. Seven years later, when Olmsted and Calvert Vaux were given the task of creating New York's Central Park, they drew their inspiration from Paxton's designs and methods, but executed them on a larger-scale. Both parks featured extensive lawns where the public might enjoy themselves.

Paxton won the competition to design London's Crystal Palace, using the methods he had developed for the construction of greenhouses at Chatsworth. The Palace would house the Great Exhibition of 1851, more formally called The Grand Exhibition of the Works of Art of All Nations. The Palace was originally set up in Hyde Park in central London, but the park in 1851 was not quite what Londoners and tourists know today.

Probably there are quite a few things that link together an electrocuted sheep in Queen Victoria's central London, a Neolithic farmer near modern Iraq in 8000 BC, the singer John Denver and the TV scriptwriter Rod Serling. They are all dead, of course, and there may be other common properties, but to my mind, lawn mowing is the most satisfactory answer. All of them play a small but telling part in the history of lawn mowing. Or rather, the mowing of lawns comes into *their* histories, as we will see later.

Several years ago, I came across an article in the *Illustrated London News*, dated 16 July 1859. Headed 'The Recent Thunderstorm, Sheep Killed By Lightning in Hyde Park', it made me aware for the first time that sheep were once widely used as live public mowers. A few enquiries revealed that there were sheep in Kensington Gardens as recently as the 1920s, still keeping the grass down. I made a note of this curiosity, and moved on. Later, I set out to find the truth of the matter, and uncovered even more mower sheep.

The presence of a sheep in the middle of the world's largest city may strike some as odd at first sight—it certainly struck me that way. By the time of the lightning strike, more and more of Britain's wool was coming from the colonies, mainly Australia and New Zealand, and forward-thinking people were already planning refrigerated ships that would carry frozen lamb, hogget and mutton (and beef) to England from the colonies and South America. Britain had started to outsource its sheep farming.

In fact, the frizzled Hyde Park sheep was one of a select but not unique group. There were other sheep given the same mowing task on Woodrow Wilson's White House lawn in 1918. As they dotted the Presidential lawn, they were dedicated organic lawn croppers, expected to keep the grass short and neat. But while twentieth century park animals were only set to trim the lawns in wartime, the nineteenth century managers of Hyde Park did it because it was the norm before the lawn mowers took over.

Now we need to look back 10,000 years to the Neolithic farmers who first began to practise agriculture. When they began harvesting grain, and even more when they began deliberately planting grain seed, these farmers used a flint sickle to cut individual ears of grain off their stalks—an early form of mowing, with the bounty carried off in baskets or cloths for processing.

The flint sickles were small and short, suitable only for lopping off the grain-rich tops of the stalks. Once iron became more common, iron sickles like that on old Communist banners and the USSR flag, could be beaten out by any old blacksmith. These could be used to cut stalks close to the ground; back-breaking work. Still, when the speakers of Old English went to mow a meadow, they would have set out with sickles, not scythes.

Those who used the sickle and the scythe to harvest grain and hay were feeding themselves, those who mow lawns now are people who can feed themselves far more easily. They have no need to engage in manual labour to obtain food, and they probably cannot eat the chemical-tainted grass that is found in most lawns, yet they invest huge amounts of time, money and effort in cultivating the inedible grass. If any other animal acted so strangely, we would marvel at its behavioural disorders. If a primitive society acted this way, flocks of anthropologists would gather to sit in the trees, preening and preparing to write learned discourses.

Perhaps even one discourse would be excessive, but it is still an interesting question: how did this lawn habit come to be? There are several strands to the answer, and one is to be found in the history of the lawn mower, and the English enthusiasm for gardens—though any careful look will find that most nations share the same sort of enthusiasm. In Estonia, they tell you that in the Baltic states, only the Estonians truly love flowers, yet Latvia and Lithuania seem to have just as many flowers and flower shops. Every nation loves flowers, and every nation wants to believe that they do so more than their neighbours.

Much the same applies with grass as well, but let us stay with the nation that invented the lawn mower and the English landscape park.

✠ ✠ ✠

PARKS, GARDENS AND GRANDEUR

✠ ✠ ✠

Judy Woolcot's Australian scythe had a long history.
At some point, around the time when the Normans took
over England and snuffed out Old English, and well before
the Black Death carried off a goodly lump of the European
population, something happened.

Some clever person combined a crooked stick, two handles and a wickedly curved blade, and found how to stand and swing the blade in a neat sweep, close to the ground, slicing past the stalks and felling them. Mowing, real mowing, had arrived, and with it, came mowing injuries, as incautious people came too close to the scythe. That is where Rod Serling and John Denver come into the mowing story, but they can wait. For now, let us stay with Hyde Park and its sheep and other livestock.

There was a charge for entering Hyde Park in Cromwell's time. We know this because John Evelyn noted in his diary for 11 April 1653, 'I went to take the aire in Hide Park, when every coach was made to pay a shilling, and horse sixpence, by the sordid fellow who had purchased it of the State, as they were called'. The claims for payment were backed up by 'porters with long staves', but when the Stuarts took back their throne in 1660, free entry was allowed once more.

In an 1833 report on parks in London, a committee reported to King William IV about Regent's Park. They hoped that 'no mistaken regard for a small rent to be derived from pasturage will prevent a larger portion of this park being soon thrown open to the public under proper regulations'. In other words, animals were being run profitably in the parks in 1833, but some of the king's loyal subjects believed that enough was enough.

In 1841, Queen Victoria's husband, Prince Albert, had taken charge as Ranger and Keeper of Hyde Park and St James' Park in London, as well as other pasturages at Windsor. A good husbandman, he was able to realise

a profit of some £2000 a year, buying lean cattle and sheep in Wales and Devon and fattening them up, nearer to London before selling them in the open market. The Royal family had no Victorian hang-ups about entering into trade, so long as it was the farming trade.

In 1851, as London's Great Exhibition opened, *The Times* thundered about the state of the park. There were open ditches, filled with filth, and rotted railings similar to the 'hurdles' used to contain the park's sheep. *The Times* reported in 1856 that Victoria Park and Regent's Park had greatly improved by the prohibition of cattle, though sheep were still allowed.

" It is expected that those who have the power in Hyde Park will follow the example which has been set in the other parks, and that the walks and grass of Hyde Park may soon be as free from the nuisances consequent upon pasturage by cows as the other parks are. If, as it is said, there are some subordinate officers who claim a right of the 'run of a cow', let them be settled with. The day is gone by for such privileges of annoyance to the public. "

Here and there, the sheep held on. In the 1860s, on the track at Beaufort House, 'a very famous runner, Colbeck, once won a Quarter-Mile Championship, beat a record and broke the leg of an awe-stricken sheep at one and the same time'.

Woodrow Wilson's White House sheep saved manpower during the First World War. The wool from the sheep was sold to benefit the Red Cross.

Remember where the park ideal came from. Andrew Jackson Downing was behind much of the suburban lawn obsession of modern times. He regarded a badly kept lawn as the sign of a 'rude and barbarous people'. He wanted the American suburb to be a bastion of civility, unlike 'barbarous' agricultural life and life in the 'uncivil' city. Civility would be shown in a concern for kempt lawns, he said.

The public lawn ideal (as opposed to the selfish desire to have a private lawn) reached America around the time of independence, and it became well established in the earliest days of the new nation. Downing imported the nineteenth century 'aristocratic' tradition from England. He set out the principles and published them so the idea of lawn could fuse with the colonial garden tradition and be brought to life in the 1860s. Sadly, he was dead by then.

Downing had mentored and encouraged Olmsted and then introduced him to Vaux. After Downing was killed in a steamboat explosion in 1852, the other two men worked together to win the competition to design Central Park. The original specifications for Central Park included a military parade ground where the Sheep Meadow is now. Under some duress, Olmsted and Vaux included the parade ground in their design, but they believed that a public park was not the place for soldiery to strut and parade.

Later, they persuaded the park commissioners to drop the idea of a parade ground. To underline this, the peaceful sheep were introduced into the area where the soldiers had been planning to assemble. After the US Civil War, in 1865, the two men formed a partnership and began designing whole suburbs, like Chicago's Riverside.

Downing's ideal lawn required no mowing with a mechanical mower, probably because even when he died, the lawn mower was imperfect. In 1849, *Scientific American* described Downing's philosophy, which was to move away from the showy villa, greenhouse and garden and opt instead for that which was more 'captivating to the man of fine taste as a cottage embosomed in shrubbery, a little park filled with a few fine trees, a lawn kept short by a flock of favorite sheep, amid a knot of flowers woven gaily together in the green turf of the terrace under the parlor windows'.

In November 1859, *Harper's New Monthly Magazine*'s progress report on work on Central Park suggests some sort of mower was in use. It's possible that scythes were involved, but the mower in question was probably an agricultural machine that kept long grass down without making what we would now call 'lawn'. The magazine was full of admiration for Vaux and Olmsted, while also praising Downing, who had managed to increase the original 160-acre site to 773 acres (later to 843 acres).

Harper's described the finished parts of the park as being in the midst of frantic work, involving between 3000 and 4000 men, and expected to cost around US$1.7 million. All over the place, roads were being laid, rocks drilled, drains dug, trees planted, bridges built, walls laid and grass mown.

" New York at length has its crowning triumph, in which the whole country is interested. It is called the Central Park, and it consists of the vast garden which Messrs Olmsted and Vaux are creating in the centre of Manhattan island. It is a garden in the largest and most generous sense—not a series of flower-beds, but a system of avenues, drives, walks, paths, terraces, lawns, streams, falls, bridges, grottoes, tunnels, shrubberies, groves, hedges, flowers, and all that human intelligence can achieve in adorning and beautifying the earth.

The finest, hardest, blackest, most solid roads wind along the edges of the loveliest reaches of lawn, broken by groups of trees and strange, rich, luxurious tropical plants, as well as the most common, but not therefore the least lovely, of our native growths. Bridges of the most elaborate and exquisite design and ornamentation already leap the ravines and span the streams. In the Ramble there is the high finish, the polish of the most carefully kept garden. Upon whatever spot the eye falls that seems to be the spot especially elaborated.

The roads of the Central Park are wider than the widest of the Bois de Boulogne, and they will be out of sight except when not immediately under foot ... "

Downing's book *Designs for Cottage Residences* had been reviewed enthusiastically in the *New Englander and Yale Review* in November 1850. With 320 illustrations, it was commended to even those planning only a woodhouse or a barn, because of the excellent hints it offered:

> " ... He will show you an intimate connection between the shape and structure of your domicil and the deepest springs of taste and feeling, and demonstrate to you the moral and esthetic qualities of a velvet lawn or a vine covered porch. In short he will give you new ideas of what that blessed English word 'home' means, and will give home a higher place than before in your esteem. "

Clearly, the lawn ideal was alive and well, some 15 years before the Riverside development in Chicago, but it was experiencing a rational and logical development. When they finally came, Olmsted's Chicago homes were built in the age of the lawn mower and set back from the street far enough to allow room for a nice sweep of lawn in front.

These were unified lawns, apparently continuous, but divided by property lines that were respected. It was neither city nor country, offering some of each, presenting a sense of the backwoodsman's cabin in the clearing that offered all mod cons, and that was about as genuine as Marie Antoinette's advances in sheep husbandry. All the same, Marie Antoinette's mock peasant world impinged directly on the fate of American lawn.

THE JEFFERSON CONNECTION

Thomas Jefferson, third president of the United States of America, sage, polymath, friend of scientists and exponent of freedom was also a slave owner. He may also have fathered the children of a slave, Sally Hemings: the genetic evidence is good but not definite, so let us say he probably did. Let us not, however, call him guilty, for slave ownership and exploitation was normal in those days, and we cannot apply modern morals retrospectively.

What was *not* normal in Jefferson's time was an admiration of lawn, but Jefferson had succeeded Benjamin Franklin as US Ambassador to France. In 1789, he returned from Paris, where he had lived on the Champs Élysées. He had spent a great deal of time close to the best architectural sites of the city, places he explored thoroughly. When he returned home, he was inspired by what he had seen, but as a hard-working Secretary of State in Washington DC, he was limited in what he could do to copy it for his home.

Jefferson had inherited the Monticello estate from his father in 1764, and by 1768, he was having the top of the Monticello mountain levelled to build his first house there. Then in 1796, he started transforming it into its present form. When the *North American Review* published a look at Jefferson in 1835, Monticello was complete as a memorial to the former president, even though Jefferson had died in debt in 1826, forcing his family to sell up.

❝ The whole mountain, with the exception of the summit, is covered with a dense and lofty forest. On the top is an elliptic plain of about ten acres, formed by the hand of art, cutting down the apex of the mountain. This extensive artificial level is laid out in a beautiful lawn, broken only by lofty weeping willows, poplars, acacias, catalpas and other trees of foreign growth, distributed at such distances as not to obstruct the view of the centre in any direction. ❞

Jefferson planned the lawn in 1807, something we know from a surviving letter to his granddaughter, a letter which includes his original sketch plan for the lawn. By 1808, the lawn existed as a somewhat untidy surface, a favourite playing space for the children of the property. Historians think it was probably only scythed once or twice a year, and while there is a reference to sheep browsing around the orange trees in a nearby greenhouse, Jefferson would probably not have allowed sheep so close to the flowerbeds.

But if the lawn was rough in reality, the *ideal* of a smooth lawn was soon out there, as Washington Irving made clear in one of a series of essays written in 1819–20, and later made into a book, *The Sketchbook of Geoffrey Crayon*. There, we read a telling comment:

> **" Society is like a lawn, where every roughness is smoothed, every bramble eradicated, and where the eye is delighted by the smiling verdure of a velvet surface. "**

Jefferson's western lawn at Monticello is still there. The property is now in the hands of the Thomas Jefferson Foundation, and open to visitors who can walk the gravelled path around the West Lawn, admiring the flowers and enjoying the serenity which overcomes the pressure applied to this much-visited location. A few miles away, another lawn commemorates him even better.

Unlike some of his successors in office, Jefferson cared deeply about education, and also about the separation of church and state. When he directed the formation of the University of Virginia, it was inevitable that the central feature would be a library, rather than a chapel. Looking back at Monticello, we should not be surprised that the other feature of the campus was The Lawn, a name that later came to stand for the university itself.

In 1820, reviewing the plans for the new university, which had opened the previous year, the *North American Review* reported as follows:

> **" We understand from the statement of the plan of the buildings, that professors' houses, placed at proper intervals on the sides of a lawn to be left indefinitely open on one side, are to have wings consisting of what we would call one-story buildings, for the accommodation of students, two in a room. "**

In Latin, *campus* means a field, so the setting out of universities and colleges, each on its campus, was intended to convey a sense of something. The older universities like Britain's Oxford and Cambridge are mixed in with the town, but newer universities tend to be located on a campus with lawns.

That said, the older European universities also have colleges. These have pleasing quadrangles and other spaces with smooth grass. Happily, this notion crossed the Atlantic to America. Indeed, there is a belief, almost certainly a myth, that the famed Kentucky bluegrass originated as seed taken from one of the quadrangles at Oxford or Cambridge (as you might expect with a myth, there are differing versions). I can't imagine the grass on a quadrangle being allowed to run to seed, just to benefit a mere colony!

LAWNS AND PARKS

Turning back to the park makers for a moment, Paxton designed a number of other parks and even Coventry Cemetery. Most importantly, he laid out the grounds of the Crystal Palace on Sydenham Hill after it was relocated from Hyde Park, along with the Italian formal gardens, the English informal gardens, the 'hextinct hanimals' (fanciful reconstructions of dinosaurs), terraces, statuary and temples, adding new lakes and cascades. Olmsted busied himself, during the Civil War with the US Sanitary Commission, directing hospitals and facilities for sick and wounded soldiers, and in other work. Paxton died in 1865, the year that Olmsted and Vaux formed their partnership.

The line from Paxton continued into the twentieth century. In 1879, Samuel Parsons Jnr, wrote about city and country lawns in *Scribner's Monthly*. To Parsons, the 'turf' was a backdrop for the ornamental trees that were planted over it, and he could happily contemplate a turf composed of ivy in a garden, though he still favoured grass for larger lawns.

Parsons was a horticulturist and his father was the first man to import Japanese maples into the USA. He worked for some years in the family business, so we should not be too surprised that the Japanese maple rates highly in his list of suitable things to plant on a lawn. He was 35 when he wrote his article, and in the same year, branched out from horticulture when he was 'apprenticed' to Calvert Vaux for five years. He became Vaux' partner in 1887 and later went on to become a leading landscape architect himself. In 1881, Vaux gave him an unpaid position at Central Park, so as to secure Parsons' position as his successor in New York.

CENTRAL Park seems never to have
had its main lawns controlled, gnawed and trimmed
by animals. Sheep were, however, introduced into one
portion in 1864. They were set loose daily on
the Sheep Meadow until 1934, but they were mainly
there to emphasise the peaceful nature of the park,
not to mow the lawns. Still, the park might have
been covered with mowing animals if Downing had
not been killed in an accident. This is the sort of
unpredictable detail that can derail, delay or redirect
the future of a technology—though the invention
of the lawn mower was probably more important in
keeping the sheep away.

Aside from his Central Park work, Parsons designed Seward, De Witt Clinton, and Jefferson parks in New York, and from 1902, worked on what would become Balboa Park in San Diego. In 1904, he published *Landscape gardening: Notes and suggestions on lawns and lawn planting*. However you look at it, Parsons was part of a thread that started at least as far back as Paxton, passing through Downing, Olmsted and Vaux.

The park architects all looked back to William Wordsworth, who (as we will see later) had praised the conversion of a vegetable garden to a lawn. The poet believed that the beauty and power of natural scenery could enrich people's lives. To the architects, all that was needed was somebody willing to impose beauty, but a side-effect was a strengthening of Everyman's desire to own his own small slice of beauty on his suburban lot.

By 1865, the lawn mower was multiplying as new models and designs came out, steam trams and other forms of commuter transport were ready. The world was in love with its public lawns, its park lawns, its formal palace lawns. The means, the opportunity and the motive were in place and the world (or parts of it) could be seen to be ready for the home lawn. But at first, only the rich could apply.

LAWN MOWING AND CLASS

When Ronald P. Reagan, the son of the US president wanted to prove he was without pretension, he told an interviewer 'We're not rich ... I mow my own lawn'. We can see the same sort of class assumption about who does the mowing in a comment by Warren Bennis, an American management guru. He was discussing his time as President of the University of Cincinnati.

❝ I wanted to be a university president but I didn't want to do it. I wanted the influence. In the end I wasn't very good at being a president. I looked

out of the window and thought that the man cutting the lawn actually seemed to have more control over what he was doing. 99

Lawn was quickly established as a class thing in the USA. The poor might have a yard, but lawn was what the well-off had. They had it even if they were often too engaged in becoming and staying well-off to attend to fine details like actually mowing their lawns. There is still an element of class about it, and as an American friend explained, 'a lawn service around here is composed of a white boss and various immigrants of questionable legality'.

In some ways, the lawn service looks like a return of the servant class. Lawn mowing involves cash payments, making it excellent for those who are part of the 'grey economy', working independently of the taxation and welfare systems. The capital outlay is small: an old utility or pickup, a mower and a spare, fuel containers, a rake or two, a whipper snipper (or weed whacker), a leaf blower and a mobile phone so customers can call you. Then it is simply a matter of enrolling customers and calling on a regular cycle.

It is, however, a seasonal industry and one that can be affected by bad weather: in dry times, the grass does not grow, in wet times, it cannot be mown. The life of the lawn worker is not a firmly based one. More than that, there is always the risk that a rival will call around and undercut the established mowing fee.

Then there is the legend of the mower man who claimed he was paid by being allowed to 'sleep with the lady of the house'. The tale usually involves a well-off American family which happens to belong to a perceived (or assumed) lower-class minority. They move into a slightly snooty area and an Anglo neighbour, usually female, sees the male of the new arrivals mowing the lawn.

This is her first sighting of the 'mower man', because the established neighbours have been away. When the woman asks what he charges to mow the lawns, he understands her mistake and replies laconically, 'Well. it depends—this place, I get to sleep with the lady of the house'. The heroes of this tale that I have been able to identify include Thurgood Marshall, Bill Cosby, Lee Trevino, Flip Wilson and Groucho Marx, but no doubt there is at least one version circulating where the response is delivered by an Asian or Hispanic comedian.

In the past, popular sardonic lines were always attributed to Mark Twain. More recently, George Carlin became the chief attributee. One Carlinism (actually the work of Bill Maher) runs as follows:

> " Stop giving me that pop-up ad for classmates.com! There's a reason you don't talk to people for 25 years. Because you don't particularly like them! Besides, I already know what the captain of the football team is doing these days: mowing my lawn. "

A double whammy, this takes a swipe at the fleeting fame that comes from being a high school sporting hero, but also locks firmly into place the notion that mowing is a lower-class activity. The reality is a little different, as many lawn services offer professional support for the lazy love-lawn, but one thing abides: the work is always done by a man. Well, nearly always, and when it isn't done by a male, it is notable, as we will see later.

THE LAWN MAKETH THE GENTLEMAN

As the nineteenth century progressed, the ownership of lawns became the norm. We even find O Henry describing a Cherokee in 'The Atavism of John Tom Little Bear' in terms which included lawn mowing. This particular Native American wore a tie, leather shoes, and had acquired an education.

> " But for his complexion, which is some yellowish, and the black mop of his straight hair, you might have thought here was an ordinary man out of the city directory that subscribes for magazines and pushes the lawn-mower in his shirt-sleeves of evenings. "

In other words, John Little could easily pass for a denizen of one of the better suburbs. I wondered where this image of mowers and magazines originated. After some digging by my tame lawyer (who happens to be my son, Angus), I discovered an explanation of sorts: the expression is related to the notion of a 'reasonable man' in US law, unless the lawyers took it from O Henry.

In England and Australia (which derives its law from British law), this paragon of lay sanity and legal normality is known as 'the man on the Clapham omnibus', which gives us a measure of his wealth and likely address. So why does the US equivalent of this Londoner get involved with magazines and lawn mowers?

The answer turned up in what seems like an odd place at first glance. On consideration, the location makes sense when you consider the gender aspects and assumptions in the literature of lawn care, lawn mowing and even in the term 'reasonable man'. It appears in the *Journal of the National Women's Studies Association* and according to Frances Ranney:

> 66 The 'man in his shirtsleeves' was used to give concrete meaning to the image of reasonableness developed in negligence law early in the twentieth century (Ehrenreich 1210). That image, later imported into sexual discrimination law, unabashedly invokes maleness as it simultaneously attempts to appeal to ideals of tolerance and inclusiveness. This unjacketed man, who 'takes the magazines at home and in the evening pushes the lawn mower,' is clearly neither an elite nor a member of the underclass (1211). As such, the image is intended to mediate among diverse social and economic groups. But Ehrenreich argues convincingly that the image incorporates not only gender but also class hierarchies; the man in his shirtsleeves has no office at which to receive magazines and no groundskeeper to mow his lawn—though he does have a lawn. 99

As it is with the law, so it is with the lawn. The lawn and its mowing are very much the domain of the male, and a somewhat macho sort of male at that. I once had a neighbour, a puffed-up, strutting rotund peacock, who was appalled that my wife mowed the lawns with a push mower while I was inside writing. It was unseemly, he thought, for a mere woman to be seen wielding a mower, and in the end, we hired a lawn man, just to keep the peacock off our backs.

It seems worth asking, why is lawn different? Why could my neighbour's wife prune in the garden, when the lawn was off-limits? And why is it appropriate for somebody to lecture their neighbours on what is, after all, a purely domestic arrangement about our division of labour? There is something dark about lawns, lying buried deep in human psychology. Ever since they discovered fire, perhaps half a million years ago, perhaps 150,000 years ago, so between 15,000 and 5000 generations back, humans were pushed to adopt a division of labour, where some of a nomadic group needed to stay at or close to the encampment, to keep the fire alight.

Women, with small children to care for may have stayed close to the camp even before humans learned to manage fire. They would have gathered staples in the local area while men ranged further afield, catching the occasional large animal that delivered a feast for the whole family. That is the pattern in modern hunter-gatherer societies, so a division of labour could be hard-wired into us, just because this particular pattern favoured survival.

We are about 300 generations beyond the invention of agriculture, and there seem to be certain fixed and inviolable patterns of behaviour, with males taking charge of farming in pre-mechanical agricultural societies. The man ploughs, not the woman, and some fanciful types even see the plough as a phallus, making the ground bear seed. Equally, the scythe appears to be seen as 'Man's work'. Death is always depicted as a man with a scythe, and we sing 'one man went to mow, went to mow a meadow ...'

All the same, in the late nineteenth century, mowers with a 6-inch (150 mm) cut were sold as 'ladies' models', followed by boy, man, man-and-boy and even two-man models about 20 inches (500 mm) across. There were also donkey mowers at 22 inches (550 mm), pony mowers at 30 inches (750 mm) and horse mowers at 36 inches (900 mm).

It cannot have been a complete taboo for women to mow, because many nineteenth century mower advertisements stress that they are suitable for girls or women. They are usually accompanied by pictures of pretty women showing a lot of leg and wielding a mower with a happy smile. Then again, psychologists and novelists of a certain type will tell you that nothing is quite so titillating to the male of the species as the hint of a taboo being broken.

✾ ✾ ✾

THE LAWN IMPERATIVE

✻ ✻ ✻

In many ways, the lawn is an unfair imposition, an intolerable burden, whether men or women take it on. A 1981 poll in the USA indicated that four out of five Americans were dissatisfied with their lawn, based as it was on inappropriate European grasses that needed constant watering, fertiliser and mowing to look ideal.

The same grasses were coopted to suit the purposes of Australian suburbanites, but under even harsher conditions. Poet Dorothea Mackellar described Australia as 'a land of drought and flooding rains', but the rains can be months or even years apart, and a city of four million like Sydney needs to have enough water storage to last ten years of average use. For much of this century, that city's gardeners and lawn lovers have been under water restrictions.

True, we might blame the lawn obsession on our recent agricultural ancestry, but it may be older than that. Our ancestors lived and developed into recognisable humans, surrounded by the East African savannah, over a period that began maybe 5 million years ago. We only left there about 150,000 years ago, so 97% of our life was spent in low grasslands. Could that be part of it?

Against that, the grass of the savannah is long and wavy, and any predecessor who liked grass long enough to conceal a large cat was probably not a contributing ancestor of the modern human gene pool. We know that evolution works on biological traits, but it works even faster against stupidity.

Related to this, another theory is that in recent times, people liked a clear field of fire that any attackers would need to come through. The manor lawns of Europe and Britain became prestigious, a clear assertion that one had 'arrived', and was important or wealthy enough to be worth attacking. The point is that you can make up suppositions and just-so stories until the cows come home

(OK, Mr Veblen, so long as they are not on the front lawn!), but they can only be suppositions. The fact remains that our society likes neat lawns. The instinct was there before Olmsted, but he made an institution of it.

The USA and Australia are both at least superficially less caught up with a class system and a sense of class than Britain. Even so, in these two radically egalitarian English-speaking nations, the less well-off are still dragged into the lawn care maelstrom. It seems that those with money need to attend to the outward appearances, if only by proxy. Can it be that everybody in those two societies must, in the absence of class, be regarded as upper class, and so entitled to a mini-estate?

The Englishman's home may be his castle, but what is the American's, or the Australian's home? Perhaps it is their lawn. Given the way many of them defend their lawns, Australians and Americans seem to be convinced that the lawn is very much part of their territory, and to be defended as such.

While I was chasing lawns in Dover, Delaware, I came across this definition of a civil trespass action in that state:

> **" A civil trespass action involves the wrongful, intentional, or negligent actions of a person that resulted in damage to another's property. For example, damages caused by an improper act of another person may involve an automobile as a result of a traffic accident, to a home, lawn, bicycle, or to any other personal property. "**

So there you have it: in Delaware, stay off the citizen's lawn! Sometimes the courts become even more closely involved in the aftermath of a defence. In Union Township, Ohio, outside Cincinnati in March 2006, Charles Martin, then aged 66, calmly waited for a 15-year-old neighbour. The boy had walked across Martin's lawn while on his way to play basketball, and when warned to stay off, he had answered back.

According to Martin later, there was more to the story. In his version of the events, Larry Mugrage Jr. had been deliberately goading and harassing him. Martin added that the boy's family and friends had also joined in the fun.

Martin's single-storey home was described later as having a neat lawn, well-trimmed shrubbery and a flagpole with US and US Navy flags flying from it. Others called the lawn 'patchy', but it was Martin's pride and joy nonetheless. While he was generally liked, his neighbours noticed that he obsessed over his lawn, getting into a rage on one occasion when a neighbour mowed one foot over the invisible boundary that marked out Martin's lawn.

When the boy walked on his lawn that last time, Martin went into his house, loaded a shotgun, and waited in front of it for the boy to return. As he walked across Martin's lawn for his last time, the man shot him from the house, injuring him. Then he walked up to the prone boy and shot him again before he went inside and calmly called the police to report 'I just killed a kid'.

In court, before he was sentenced to at least 18 years in jail, Martin said he was sorry for shooting the boy, but added that Larry Mugrage knew that he cared about his lawn, and deliberately provoked him. 'He stepped on it and he walked 40 feet through it,' Martin said. 'I cared about it. I cut it every five days.'

The killer was tried on a charge of aggravated murder, but in the end, the jury took less than four hours to convict him on the lesser count of murder because they could not agree about whether or not the killing was planned. His lawyer had conceded that Martin shot Mugrage, but argued that the man had been harassed for some years by Mugrage and other neighbourhood youths who insulted the man and ignored his pleas to stay off the lawn.

A DEADLY WATER FIGHT

If lawn lovers can kill, lawn lovers can also die. In late 2007, a Sydney grandfather died of a heart attack after a row over water restrictions. Todd Munter, 36, apparently saw Ken Proctor, 66, watering his lawn with a hose. At the time, there were restrictions on the hours when hoses could be used, but Proctor was watering his lawn within the permitted period using a hand-held hose.

Munter was alleged to have called Proctor a 'stupid old goat', apparently because he thought the grandfather was breaking the water restrictions. When Proctor turned his hose on Munter, the younger man was reported to have first punched him, and then pushed him to the ground and kicked him. Passers-by, including an off-duty police officer intervened, and an ambulance was called, but Proctor, a retired truck driver, suffered a massive heart attack and died in hospital, soon after.

Australia was in the sixth year of a severe drought and most parts of the nation had restrictions on water use. Garden sprinklers were banned, hard surfaces could not be washed with hoses, and gardens and lawns could only be watered at specified times on certain days. People caught breaching the regulations were fined. Proctor, however, was not in breach.

Evidence was given in an earlier hearing that Munter had been on medication for a chronic back problem for four-and-a-half years, but that he was not suffering from any mental health problems at the time of the attack, and he was charged with murder. In mid-December 2008 Munter pleaded guilty to manslaughter in the New South Wales Supreme Court. At the time of printing, Munter was on conditional bail awaiting sentencing.

After a while, stories like this are embellished by tabloid journalists. This is why you need to wonder about all sorts of tales, anecdotes and theories—and their origins. For example, could it have been confetti makers who spread the false yarn that rice scattered over a bride and groom endangers the lives of birds which later ate the grain? The rumour said that birds are attracted to the grain as it lies on the grass, they eat it, the rice grains absorb water and swell up, causing the birds to explode. They don't, not according to the USA Rice Federation in Houston, Texas.

IN the nineteenth century, when death rates in ordinary civilian life were so much higher than today, fancy burials and even fancier tombs and headstones were the order of the day. Fearsome angels, broken columns and other symbols decorated the graveyards. Graves had iron rails, raised mounds, flowerbeds and more, but in the mid-1850s, just a short time before the lawn mower emerged, people began looking for a simpler, cleaner line, and so the concept of the lawn cemetery came into being, an area that could be scythed into neatness.

Then again, they would say that, wouldn't they? True, they would, but in this case, they know what they are saying. At Humpty Doo in Australia, a rice-growing scheme went bankrupt when magpie geese ate the crop, and no magpie geese were seen exploding. In Texas, migratory birds commonly eat a part of the crop. Uncooked rice on the stalk is no more and no less dangerous than uncooked rice on the lawn.

On the other hand, confetti on the lawn, is quite a problem, because it is almost impossible to pick up. Not even a lawn vacuum will get it out of the grass, where the wet paper can mat and cause a degree of clogging. If confetti lands on a hard surface and gets wet, the paper pieces can be a bit slippery, but rice on a hard surface is much more dangerous, since clumsy, elderly and/or inebriated relatives (traditional at weddings in some countries) may slip on the hard round rice grains.

Then there is the strange belief that half-empty clear plastic bottles of water lying on a lawn will somehow stop dogs fouling it. There may need to be four or five bottles on a biggish lawn, but people will swear by the remedy. There has been no controlled study of this, and obviously people who see no effect are less likely to report back than those who think it works.

The use of bottles in this way is common in the USA, Britain, Canada, Australia, New Zealand, and Japan, so either it works, or people in many lawn-loving cultures are gullible. Who would believe that people who are willing to devote vast amounts of money and much of their leisure time to the pointless culture of a sterile biological desert to impress passers-by could ever be judged as gullible?

There are quite a few possible explanations for this, ranging from dogs not wanting to foul the area near water, to the glint of the bottle (or the sight of their reflection) alarming the dogs in some way, or some sort of smell. More probably, if the method does work, it is because dog owners see the bottles as a warning that a clean-lawn zealot may pursue and humiliate them in public if they don't clean up after their dog. For my part, dog droppings are small and they degrade, they discourage people from walking on the grass, they provide soil nutrients, and they are a long way less ugly than half a dozen half-empty clear plastic bottles glinting in the sun!

IN ANOTHER COUNTRY

One thing seems to distinguish Australia, parts of New Zealand and the USA from the rest of the world: the street lawn. A Norwegian friend tells me that even in Scandinavia, spring also brings the sound of lawn mowers, but these are applied to parks and small enclosed plots only.

As in so many other things, Australia is a sort of average between Britain and the USA, sometimes leaning more to one, sometimes leaning more to the other. Australian suburban homes have front lawns, usually with a fence. Then there is the 'nature strip', a portion of grass, far from natural, which is on the public street, between the fence and the roadside kerb, an area that the attentive home-owner is expected to keep neat and trim, though the pressure to do so is more moral than the sort of legal requirement some Americans know.

As I have already explained in the introduction, our home computers can bring us satellite images at a good enough resolution to reveal the streetscapes of different towns in different places. We can see these nature strips, the unnatural portions of grass beyond the front fence in suburban Australia and New Zealand, generally with a concrete footpath near the fence. Having said that, the grass strips in New Zealand are called verges.

Britain lacks these grassy edges but the US has them in most suburbs, generally without any sidewalk, as a footpath is called there. My American informants tell me that the space has a number of regional names, including the 'right of way', the parking strip, the devil's strip and the parkway. The discussion that followed revealed that many Americans don't know what it is called elsewhere in America. We did, however, spot one major difference: the roadside grass is private property in the USA, but public property in Australia and New Zealand. In each country, though, the grass is treated as though it were owned.

THE ART OF THE ASTROTURF

The street lawn is stoutly defended, and sometimes, the instinct to do so is exploited. On occasions, politicians and commercial firms engage in a form of trickery known as Astroturfing. This involves setting up an apparent grass roots campaign which has as much to do with the real grass roots as Astroturf has to do with the figurative grass roots.

That said, there was a time when the Astroturfing ploy was all about lawn and the love of it. A yarn was circulated on the internet in 2004, when John Edwards was the candidate for the Democratic vice-presidential nomination in the USA. Like all damaging propaganda, it was largely false, but contained a few elements of truth (lawn had been damaged) surrounded by a great deal of spin.

It took the form of an email that began: 'I'd like to introduce you to my neighbor. I'm from Raleigh, North Carolina, and for several years I've lived around the corner from Vice Presidential Candidate John Edwards. My neighbor John has been in the news a good deal lately, but it's hard to tell about the man himself from the coverage. Maybe I can help you get to know him better'.

In a neat piece of demolition, Edwards was then accused of being aloof and not mixing with the neighbours. Later enquiries among actual neighbours showed that the community activities he supposedly avoided simply did not exist. After several other accusations came the master blow of the email: it said that in January 2003, Edwards had arranged matters so that media trucks were forced to park on lawns near his house when he announced his presidential bid. The message was clear: John Edwards was un-American: *he did not care about other people's lawns*!

On went the attack: 'I heard two families ended up re-sodding their damaged yards, and John never apologized to anyone, much less offered any compensation. The family across the street from my neighbor John has since put up posts at their property line to try to keep that sort of thing from happening again'.

When the *Raleigh News and Observer* looked into the claims, a rather different story emerged. Edwards had not behaved as described, and where the letter claimed that Edwards had never offered compensation for lawn damage, either Edwards or his team were a little more savvy than that: on the same day he made his announcement that he was running for president, he offered both an apology and an offer to pay for repairs! After apologizing for 'any inconvenience you and your family may have experienced', Edwards wrote (or his minders wrote on his behalf):

> 66 Please call our assistant, Andrew Young ... if you have any lawn damage from the media traffic. Our personal lawn maintenance company will make any necessary repairs. Thank you for your patience. 99

The damage, however, was probably done. Any right-thinking lover of lawns would have got the message that one presidential candidate was a man who did not care about his neighbour's lawn rights. He simply wasn't a proper person! In a political system where the two candidates or two teams are running neck and neck, a grass roots lawn rights whispering campaign can make all the difference, just so long as the lawn lovers don't detect the smell of the Astroturf!

AUSTRALIAN LAWN

Australian outback roads have grassy verges, often referred to as 'the shoulder'. In the Kimberley region of tropical north-west Australia, I spoke to the driver of a bulldozer that had been modified to drag a large mowing machine along the shoulder. I asked him why it seemed necessary to mow the edges. I did not raise the conservation issue, but I was thinking of the role played by British hedgerows, which shelter a great deal of wildlife, and provide fodder for farm animals in harsh times.

It turned out that I was right about wildlife sheltering on the verges. The driver volunteered the information that having wildlife close to the road meant more roadkills, which attracted carrion-eaters, and caused even more roadkills. Having fodder beside the road attracted large kangaroos, some as heavy as a man. These were not only killed when they were hit, but the collisions damaged vehicles. The fodder also attracted large feral mammals and, depending on where you were, a vehicle might run into, kill and be damaged by, feral goats, pigs, donkeys, horses or camels. To save animal and human lives, mowing was essential.

Grass was an important consideration in the first European settlement of Australia. When James Cook sailed H.M. Bark *Endeavour* into Botany Bay in April 1770, he had two botanists on board, Joseph Banks and Daniel Solander. The two men and their assistants collected many plants, and even that late in the southern autumn, would still have found a few in flower.

They were good collectors, but ignorant about agriculture, so when Banks saw patches of green some distance from the coast, he was rhapsodic about the fine meadows that were there, just waiting for canny British farmers to begin mowing them. He persuaded Cook to change the bay's original name, Stingray Harbour, to Botany Bay, and back in England, he sang his praises of Botany Bay as a fine and very suitable place to settle a British colony.

Banks soon became Sir Joseph Banks, a favourite of King George III, and was elected president of the Royal Society. Using that position and the power of royal favour, he urged a settlement, and when some uppity Americans decided to cut their ties with Mother England, leaving Britain nowhere to dump its surplus felons, Banks and his supporters seized their chance. In 1787, a small fleet (the 'First Fleet' of Australian history books), set sail from England, arriving at Botany Bay in January, 1788.

That was the height of Australia's high summer, a time of year when lawn mowers are now heard either early in the morning, or as night descends, because it is too hot in the middle of the day to cut the grass. Water was probably scarce in that first January, but when the 'meadows' of Botany Bay were examined, they turned out to be no better than dismal swamps, overlying barren sandy soil. There would be no pastures here, there would be no hay cut. The future of the colony was at risk, so Governor Phillip moved the colony a few miles north to Sydney.

For most of the nineteenth century, Australians cared about grass only as feed for stock. Grass, they found, goes brown in summer, and that knowledge even crept into one of the more popular Australian Christmas carols—but the grass in question is defined as being in 'the paddock', the normal Australian term for a field. The state of grass around an Australian house was not a matter of serious concern, and given the nature of Australian summers, nobody was going to put much effort into trying to tend it. Grand houses might feature one, but a lawn was not within the aspirations of ordinary Australians.

The croquet lawn was certainly a feature of the houses of those who felt superior. In 1871, Rachel Henning settled in Australia and wrote an extensive set of letters which survived her. She reported in one, with apparent pleasure, that her brother had wooed his future wife on a Sydney croquet lawn.

We may reasonably assume, however, that the upkeep and maintenance of the lawn was left to servants; in the hands of the hands, you might say. In that era, it would not have done for the better people who owned property to be seen mowing, sweeping, weeding or rolling the green. That was for suburbanites, and the US-style suburbs had yet to reach the Antipodes.

Writing in *Oceana, or England and Her Colonies* in 1886, J.A. Froude gave a traveller's view of Australia. In it, he noted the 'clean-mown and carefully-watered lawn, with tennis-ground and croquet-ground' at Ercildoun, a grazing property near Ballarat in Victoria. This gave him the sense of having arrived at 'an English aristocrat's country house reproduced in another hemisphere'.

An Australian correspondent tells me that the tennis-ground is now asphalt, but no longer a suitable playing surface. I wondered whether it might have been so in Froude's time, but Froude was remarkably fastidious about lawns. He spent just ten weeks in Australia and New Zealand during 1885, but clearly was on the look-out for impressive lawns and gardens during his travels and jotted notes about them.

The bungalows of Adelaide, he said, '... were low, generally of one storey, shaded with large india-rubber trees, the fronts festooned with bougainvilleas, the hedges of purple tamarisk, and the small garden bright with oleanders and scarlet geraniums', but he was less impressed with the Adelaide Botanic Gardens, where he '... missed two things only: for our delicate grass there is buffalo-grass, whose coarse fibre no care in mowing can conceal ...'

A small note: common names can lead to confusion. The grass known in Australia as buffalo grass, *Stenotaphrum secundatum*, is a West Indies grass known in America as St Augustine. It is not to be confused with the US buffalo grass, *Buchloe dactyloides*. That is a native grass, found across large parts of the plains of the USA. The American grass got its name because it was the main food of the American buffalo. Folklore has it that *Stenotaphrum* was first carried to Australia on a ship called *Buffalo*.

One thing is certain: Froude hated the buffalo grass, and a name change would not have helped. He was put up at Government House in Melbourne, where he found 'the usual lawn-tennis ground', and he complained of how the 'coarse buffalo-grass eats, like a destroying monster, into its delicate English rival and kills it out of the way'. Still, anywhere with lawns was, to Froude's eye, a delight. He visited Sydney's Royal Botanic Gardens and wrote later: 'The ground slopes from the town to the sea with inclining lawns, flower-beds, and the endless variety of the tropical flora'.

LAWNS AND LITERATURE

In 1885, lawns in Australia were still either a mark of the class-conscious Briton in Australia, or of the Australian who called Britain 'home', and aped English manners, gentility, speech, fashion and dress in a very different climate. It was a time of change, though. Native-born Australians might be seen as rude and uncouth, but at the end of the nineteenth century, writers began to express an Australian spirit, and Australians began to mutter among themselves that England must be a terrible place, because the convicts came from there.

So, curiously, keeping a household lawn of the sort that might grace an English mansion or superior bungalow came into suburban fashion in Australia just when thinking Australians were starting to object to Britain and to things British, at least in literature. Politically and militarily, Australia was still profoundly British in its orientation and sympathies, but as part of the British Empire, not as a part of England. There were those who were beginning to feel that the English need not and should not, be their masters—or that if they *were* to be Australia's masters, then Australian Jack was still as good as his English master. Consider the strongly Australian writer Joseph Furphy, fulminating in 1903, about a certain style of fiction:

❝ And it is surely time to notice the threepenny braggadocio of caste ... which makes a party of resourceful bushmen stand helpless in the presence of flood or fire, till marshalled by some hero of the croquet lawn ... ❞

In 1904, in Dorothea Mackellar's famous poem 'My Country' she described the English as lovers of field, coppice, ordered woods and gardens, in contrast to her own love, the sunburnt country that is Australia. Yet while generations of schoolchildren can recite at least the second verse, somewhere along the way, a love of ordered and regimented lawns became part of the Australian dream.

American poets saw grass and lawn differently and celebrated it fulsomely. Walt Whitman could write, 'I believe a leaf of grass is no less than the journey-work of the stars', while James Russell Lowell wrote, 'In creating, the only hard thing's to begin; a grass-blade's no easier to make than an oak'. Whitman also wrote in 'Song of Myself':

> **" A child said What is the grass? fetching it to me with full hands;**
> **How could I answer the child? I do not know what it is any more than he.**
> **I guess it must be the flag of my disposition, out of hopeful green stuff woven.**
> **Or I guess it is the handkerchief of the Lord,**
> **A scented gift and remembrancer designedly dropped,**
> **Bearing the owner's name someway in the corners,**
> **that we may see and remark, and say Whose? "**

The amateur poets of nineteenth century America mainly used 'lawn' as a rhyme for 'morn' or 'dawn' in idyllic waffles about lawn as some sort of heaven on earth, cool in the sun, green, sweet and in their bucolic fantasies, free of all suggestion of weeds, prickles or bald patches caused by pests lurking in the soil. The English amateurs were just as bad, and out of kindness to the reader, will not be quoted. Those who wrote Australia's poetry before about 1920 displayed little enthusiasm for lawns and their surrounds. Like Dorothea Mackellar, they were far more likely to be excited by 'the bush', 'the outback', sandhills and the parched country of the inland.

I have found just one poetic reference to lawn in nineteenth century Australasian poetry: New Zealander Johannes Carl Andersen mentioned a lawn in 'Soft, low and sweet', but this was a daisy lawn. In 'An Evening', Australian poet Dora Wilcox referred to a 'grassy lawn', in a collection published in 1918. This, however, was a mourning poem for a dead soldier whose shadow would fall no more on grassy lawn and garden wall.

Australia became, at least in name, an independent nation in 1901, though the British Foreign Office continued trying to direct Australia's policy, objecting to the visit of the US 'White Fleet' to Sydney in 1908. One voluble objector to the visit was the undersecretary of state for the colonies, one Winston Churchill, who apparently had trouble distinguishing an independent nation from a colony. He declared that the American visit '… ought certainly to be discouraged from every point of view'. The visit was part of a complicated chess game which led to Australia establishing its own navy in 1911 and taking charge of its own foreign policy.

The Froudes of Britain, with their distaste for Australian grasses and the Churchills of Britain, with their contempt for Australian sovereignty, go a long way to explaining the attitudes that Joseph Furphy demonstrated, but it was only a veneer of annoyance on the part of the Australians.

When World War I broke out in 1914, Australia's brand new navy and Australia's young men rushed to defend the empire, where many of them died in hare-brained schemes, some of them dreamed up by the same Winston Churchill. One of these, the Gallipoli fiasco, forged an Australian character but also gave Australia the tradition or myth that the British, and British officers in particular, were not fit to lead Australians. The losers, officers and men, British and colonial, were buried where they fell.

When the survivors returned home, it was to a nation where people were flocking to the cities, where the cities were expanding and served well by transport systems that allowed workers to return home to their dream, a home on a 'quarter-acre block' (often a bit smaller but still called that), a block with gardens—and lawns. The ones who did not return had their lawns as well, but these were in scrupulously tended war cemeteries in places like Flanders and Gallipoli. No doubt Carl Sandburg had lawn cemeteries in mind when he wrote:

> **" Pile the bodies high at Austerlitz and Waterloo.**
> **Shovel them under and let me work.**
> **I am the grass. I cover all. "**

After the US Civil war, lawn cemeteries became common, and it is likely that this time, the lawn mower played a part in the decision. Markers were small and generally flush with the ground, allowing the mower to clear away much of the overgrowth that might otherwise interpose itself.

On a side note, the American cultural historian Paul Fussell argued that the Australian upper-middle-class imitation of British ways could also be encountered in America. In his delightful book *Class*, he commented acidly on the Americans who had house names like 'The Willows': 'There's almost no limit to how cute you can be here, especially if you are upper-middle-class and fancy British usages'. Then he opens up with all guns:

> **"** Approaching any house, one is bombarded with class signals. The serious student will not panic but will take them one at a time. The lawn first. Its very existence is an announcement of Anglophilia, England being the place where the lawn came into its own. Finicky neatness here is usually a sign of social anxiety, a tip-off that we are approaching middle-class premises. If there's no crabgrass at all, we can infer an owner who spends much of his time worrying about slipping down a class or two, the lawn being, as Brooks notes, 'a crucial arena for classical predatory invidiousness and its concomitant, anxiety'. **"**

Perhaps people gave up the ornate nineteenth century tomb ornaments because of the cost involved, but they may equally have been persuaded that a dead relative deserved the simplicity of an upper-class lawn for Eternity.

❊ ❊ ❊

LAWN, STATUS AND AUTHORITY

✳ ✳ ✳

The joyous way living people adopted lawn, and their willingness to shoulder the mowing burden, poses a puzzle. How many rational males would willingly take a gentle walk, and in their perambulations, fill a large sack with rocks and carry it with them? It is one thing to mow unkempt grass to reduce a fire hazard or to deny hiding places to vermin, but lawn was a whole new game, and an onerous one. Where is the logic in turning leisure time to hard labour?

Lawn love arose from an early form of brainwashing. People who would need to mow their own lawn absorbed too many passing references to lawns, casual comments that made mowing and all of the rest sound normal. Lawns were taken as 'givens' in all sorts of circumstances.

It was understood that the lawn was very desirable and went quite a way in enhancing the status of the owner, because all the very best people had lawns. On 1 June 1799, Britain's Royal family dined in six marquees on the lawn, facing the river Thames in London. The marquees adjoined, and had tables 'spread for the Nobility', or so reported the fawning reporter of *The Times*. The message was that lawn was a suitable setting for royalty and nobility, but there was more. Six days later, a number of members of the royal family went to breakfast with the Princess of Wales, and while the courtiers were dining, the band of the London Militia played martial airs on the lawn, said *The Times*. Clearly, lawns were a mark of having arrived.

David Hessayon, writing as Dr D.G. Hessayon, has written a number of books since 1959 with titles like *The Rose Expert*, *The Tree and Shrub Expert* and *The House Plant Expert*, but his lasting fame came from *The Lawn Expert*. In this work, he made the distinction between 'utility' lawns and 'luxury' lawns. A utility lawn was there to serve a useful purpose, and might well produce hay, but a luxury lawn would have drawn the applause of Mr Veblen.

In the nineteenth century, most American farmers couldn't afford a lawn, but there must have been a few New England farmers trying, going by the comments in the *New Englander and Yale Review* in November 1860:

> **" For a man who is thoroughly in earnest, farming offers a grand field for effort; but the man who is only half in earnest, who thinks that costly barns, and imported stock, and smooth fences, and a nicely rolled lawn are the great objects of attainment, may accomplish pretty results, but they will be small ones. So the dilettante farmer who has a smattering of science, whose head is filled with nostrums, who thinks his salts will do it all; who doses a crop now to feebleness, and now to an unnatural exuberance; who dawdles over his fermentations while the neighbors' oxen are breaking into his rye-field; who has no managing capacity,—no breadth of vision,—who sends two men to accomplish the work of one,—let such a man give up all hope of making farming a lucrative pursuit. "**

By the mid-nineteenth century, anybody who was anybody in Britain had to have a lawn and all of the bright and famous seemed to have lawns. It has to be said that the idols back then were slightly different from the 'celebs' people admire today. Poets were particularly prized and admired, and the best of them could even do quite well out of poetry.

William Wordsworth favoured and praised lawns, as we can see in his poem, 'This Lawn a Carpet All Alive', written in 1829 and first published 1835, five years after Budding invented his mower, a clear warning that we should not expect too much from the poet's lawn. It mattered little, because a widely admired poet's endorsement of lawn would have been enough to inspire many people to embrace lawnism.

> **" This Lawn, a carpet all alive**
> **With shadows flung from leaves—to strive**
> **In dance, amid a press**
> **Of sunshine, an apt emblem yields**
> **Of Worldlings revelling in the fields**
> **Of strenuous idleness;**
>
> **Less quick the stir when tide and breeze**
> **Encounter, and to narrow seas**
> **Forbid a moment's rest;**
> **The medley less when boreal Lights**
> **Glance to and fro, like aery Sprites**
> **To feats of arms addrest!**
>
> **Yet, spite of all this eager strife,**
> **This ceaseless play, the genuine life**
> **That serves the steadfast hours,**
> **Is in the grass beneath, that grows**
> **Unheeded, and the mute repose**
> **Of sweetly-breathing flowers. "**

The 'sweetly-breathing flowers' may be a hint that this was no manicured, cropped, weeded and controlled spread of a single species of grass. Still, to William Wordsworth, it was quite a step up from what had preceded it, as he revealed in notes that were added to the poem when it was published:

" This lawn is the sloping one approaching the kitchen-garden, and was made out of it. Hundreds of times have I watched the dancing of shadows amid a press of sunshine, and other beautiful appearances of light and shade, flowers and shrubs. What a contrast between this and the cabbages and onions and carrots that used to grow there on a piece of ugly-shaped unsightly ground! **"**

Clearly, Wordsworth had no need to grow his own food, and his was what Veblen would have called a luxury lawn. The best thing that poets had going for them in their dealings with fans was that in those days before paparazzi, their faces were unknown. Then the rot set in. Alfred Tennyson (he only became Baron Tennyson in 1884) had a neighbour on the Isle of Wight, Julia Cameron, who began taking photographs of him in 1863. Before long, he complained to her that her 'confounded photographs' deprived him of his anonymity. When he was on his home turf, there was no way of avoiding the pests, as *Scientific American* reported in 1864 in 'The Penalties of Fame':

" The great English poet Tennyson is exposed to great annoyance from the curiosity of intruders. Strangers are found from time to time seated in his garden; peering in at his windows, wandering freely through his grounds. From the lawn in front, when conversing with his family in assumed privacy, he has, on casually looking up, discovered an enterprising British tourist taking mental notes of his conversation from the branches of a tree above. Mr Tennyson has been compelled to make fences, raise embankments, train foliage, and in fact half fortify his house, and in spite of all is not permitted to enjoy what any of our readers so circumstanced would expect to enjoy as a thing of course—the quiet freedom of a country home. **"**

When you read the authors of the Victorian era, an acceptance and appreciation of lawns appears over and over again. In 1863, Nathaniel Hawthorne described his recent sojourn in London in *The Atlantic Monthly*:

" A friend had given us his suburban residence, with all its conveniences, elegancies, and snuggeries,—its drawing-rooms and library, still warm and bright with the recollection of the genial presences that we had known there,—its closets, chambers, kitchen, and even its wine-cellar, if we could have availed ourselves of so dear and delicate a trust,—its lawn and cozy garden-nooks, and whatever else makes up the multitudinous idea of an English home,—he had transferred it all to us, pilgrims and dusty wayfarers, that we might rest and take our ease during his summer's absence on the Continent.

The garden included that prime feature of English domestic scenery, a lawn. It had been levelled, carefully shorn, and converted into a bowling-green, on which we sometimes essayed to practise the time-honored game of bowls, most unskilfully, yet not without a perception that it involves a very pleasant mixture of exercise and ease, as is the case with most of the old English pastimes. "

Just as Tennyson had his lawn, Charles Dickens had a lawn as well, at Gad's Hill, Gravesend, near London. Dickens was as much a performer of his works as he was a writer, and he conceived much of his dialogue by speaking it in front of a mirror. Many of Dickens' works were serialised, and given the way his fans waited for news of the fate of characters like Little Nell, there would no doubt have been spies lurking in the undergrowth if they had the chance, waiting to catch the dialogue that revealed the plot of the latest masterpiece, so he worked in the summer-house in his garden, safe from prying ears.

On 13 June 1859, Dickens wrote to his daughter Mamie, 'One of the balustrades of the destroyed old Rochester Bridge has been (very nicely) presented to me by the contractor for the works, and has been duly stonemasoned and set up on the lawn behind the house. I have ordered a sundial for the top ...'

The bridge at Rochester dated back to 1387, so it was indeed an acquisition. Sundials were in fashion just then, as we can see from this praise of them from *Scientific American* in 1858:

> ❝ The sundial, the oldest method of ascertaining the solar time, is always an ornament, as well as useful in a garden or on a lawn, and we are often asked by correspondents how one can be made. It is simply a circular plate having a piece rising from it, as seen in the accompanying illustration, and the hours marked on the dial. A mirror should also be inserted, to reflect and show the direction of the clouds. ❞

When Dickens died in 1870, James Fields (a writer and publisher, and at the time, the editor of the *Atlantic Monthly*) recalled Dickens playing lawn bowls at Gad's Hill:

> ❝ In that beautiful retreat he has for many years been accustomed to welcome his friends, and find relaxation from the crowded life of London. On the lawn playing at bowls, in the Swiss summer-house charmingly shaded by green leaves, he always seemed [to spend] the best part of summer, beautiful as the season is in the delightful region where he lived. ❞

LAWN GRANDEUR

We humans have a strange attachment to the places our ancestors came from. Think of the number of Americans (including presidents) who have visited Ireland and claimed Irish ancestry. Almost as many have laid claim to Scots ancestry, and Australians, New Zealanders and Canadians are no different. So if there was a subliminal message coming through that gentlemen of the British kind had lawns, other English-speakers in colonies and former colonies would fall under a temptation to emulate them.

Then there is the official lawn, intended to be imposing, to carry a message to all who look on it, a message of majesty. The major buildings of government, culture and religion are commonly set out with lawns to mark them out as special places of power. The lawns speak to us of authority and control, just as the towering spires and domes do. Churches and temples seem to use lawn less, but government and culture need lawn on their side.

In Washington DC, the centre of power is the White House lawn, while in Britain, the high and mighty mingle with their lessers at garden parties, held on lawns. The Peace Palace, the site of the United Nations International Court of Justice in The Hague is surrounded by lawn, to make the building and what it stands for, seem even grander.

A.J. Downing (he of Central Park and Chicago suburban lawn fame) redesigned the Washington Mall in 1851 as a giant lawn. He saw it linking the White House and the Capitol, making an architectural statement about the way US government should operate. He probably never thought of the Mall as a place where protest might erupt as it later did. The lawn as a symbol of grandeur became a symbol of democracy as well, and no pun intended, grass-roots democracy at that. Even so, the politician given to hubris may see grandeur in a lawn, as Richard Nixon did. Here, he writes about his inauguration:

> **The memory of that scene for me is like a frame of film forever frozen at that moment: the red carpet, the green lawn, the white house, the leaden sky. The new president and his first lady.**

In 1869, in its seventh issue, *The Manufacturer and Builder* outlined a neat plan for the grounds of a two-storey house, along with a front elevation. The house was one built at Flushing, Long Island, some two years earlier, on a block 75 feet broad and 180 feet deep (about 23 x 55 metres, about the size of a modern Olympic swimming pool), with a flower bed, a 'grass plot' and a vegetable garden, capable of growing all of the vegetables for a family. These were utility grounds, not luxury grounds.

Within a few years, the grass plot would be heard of no more, supplanted by a grander lawn. In 1877, the same journal praised the social improvement that might stem from a few neat lawns:

" What a change would be wrought in the aspect of our farming districts if the gardens and dooryards, which are too frequently filled with wood-piles, heaps of rubbish, a mixture of shade-trees, weeds, and grass, were converted into a smooth lawn, with tastefully arranged fruit-trees and shrubbery. Tree culture, from the seed or from transplanting, costs but little effort and no money, and how much they add to the ornamental as well as useful! Let some farmer take the course of improvement suggested, and it would do much to educate the taste of the whole neighborhood. "

By 1879, it was a given that American people, the ones who read the more literary magazines, would have lawns. These were no rolling open expanses of grass, but artfully displayed grass with trees and shrubs dotted around without taking away the broad open spaces. Readers of *Scribner's Monthly* were encouraged to plant and plan more:

" One of the most important considerations in planting a lot is the disposition of shrubbery and trees about the lawn in a way that will secure broad, open spaces of turf. These groups of shrubbery or trees should be arranged on the more prominent curves of walks about entrance gates, or the outer boundaries of the place. The object in view will be partly to secure the above-mentioned open spaces of turf, but chiefly to vary the effects and produce sudden, unexpected views. "

Not everybody could hope for a large garden and lawn, but by 1887, *The Manufacturer and Builder* was willing to console the less well-off: '... while ample grounds about a house are desirable for many reasons, they entail burden of care and labor which the results do not always seem to repay'.

A doctor's house (note the implication of status), coyly described in 1890 as being 'within 50 miles of New York', was featured in the January 1890 *Manufacturer and Builder*. The house sat on a large lot, with

150 feet of frontage, '... giving ample room for the well-kept lawn, whereon the doctor intended to take some muscular exercise during the spring and summer months in toying with the lawn mower'. Who knows: this democratic doctor may even have 'subscribed for magazines' that he could read in his shirtsleeves when his mowing was done.

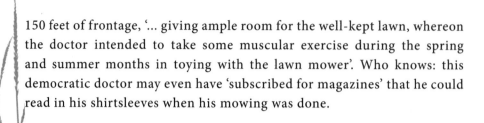

LAWN MAVERICKS

It seems that in the western world, there are three imperative chores, three tasks that are demanded of the suburbanite: doing the laundry, washing the car, and mowing the lawn. The last two are the problems: if your clothing is grubby, strangers will not comment on it, but the same strangers will write on a dirty car 'don't wash me, plant something!', and strangers will sometimes succumb to the temptation to comment that a lawn needs mowing, or even to decide to pay to have it done, as Jay Gatsby did to Nick Carraway.

> **❝ At eleven o'clock a man in a raincoat dragging a lawn-mower tapped at my front door and said that Mr Gatsby had sent him over to cut my grass. ❞**
> **F. Scott Fitzgerald, *The Great Gatsby*, chapter 5.**

Even distant neighbours who rate no higher than acquaintances may feel impelled to advise you of your lawn's needs. Sometimes, local authorities even give citizens the power to intervene when somebody in the community seems not to be conforming to standards they think are set by the community.

In the USA, some communities have had regulations in force for upwards of 100 years, forbidding home owners from having 'weeds' in their front yards, or having grass above a certain height on their property. Fines and even jail time may be handed out to offenders.

Wordsworth praised the conversion of an unsightly vegetable garden to a lawn, but about 30 years ago, the tide slowly began to turn, and something of the World War II Victory Garden movement began to re-emerge. People began to look at the transport and other costs of food, and to think about self-sufficiency. Others, with a different but equally valid ecological awareness, began to favour the deliberately unkempt but biodiverse lawn.

THE WILD LAWN

The US EPA has put together an excellent study of the case law on lawn mowing, and two cases stand out. One was in 1976, when Donald Hagar was sued by the Wisconsin City of New Berlin for violating its weed law. Hagar was a wildlife biologist, and knew his science, while the city ordinance officials were responding as only hide-bound officialdom can to a flouting of unnatural laws.

It was an uneven contest. When Hagar decided to fight City Hall, he won. They claimed that his 'natural landscape', his piece of prairie, would bring rats. Hagar produced a witness who showed that the Norway rat does not inhabit or find food in a natural landscape. The City claimed it was a fire hazard, Hagar brought in an expert witness from the United States Forest Service who testified that Hagar's prairie did not create a fire hazard.

Another expert explained that a prairie fire, unlike a forest fire, does not create large and persistent embers that can be carried by the wind, and a botanist countered the City claims that the prairie would cause pollen problems. He showed that wildflowers and natural landscapes are less of a problem for allergy sufferers. The big sources of troublesome pollen were Kentucky bluegrass, and trees, like oaks.

The court found that the factual underpinning for the weed ordinance was too thin to be rational, and so it was struck down. The city decided not to appeal, and has left natural landscapers alone since that date. One victory, however, does not make a revolution, so Walter and Nancy Stewart, a scientist and an attorney respectively, had to fight much the same battle in Maryland in 1987.

They were hit with a weed law citation when they let a six-acre natural landscape grow around their suburban home. They offered a vigorous scientific and legal argument against the Montgomery County claim that their yard gave a suitable environment for rats and snakes and released pollens that were harmful to people with respiratory problems. Faced with the Stewarts' evidence, the county dropped the charges. The weed ordinance was changed

IN the beginning, weeds were part of the lawn. Indeed, some weeds can be a benefit, though there are limits to our patience at times. The clover that offers the grass some nitrates, and provides Daisy with a small supplement of nitrogenous compounds to improve her milk can cause a slippery patch on a tennis court that will blemish the clothing with green stains, and may even give rise to broken bones, torn ligaments and strained joints. Occasionally, the price of botanical tolerance is too high.

to allow 'suburban meadows' if there is a 15-foot (5.5 metre) buffer at the edges where growth is kept down to 12 inches (30 cm), and provided that noxious weeds like poison ivy are controlled.

There have been other cases as well, but the general thrust has been that such ordinances are going to be more and more difficult to sustain. All the same, there are still rules out there. The city of East Lansing ('The Home of Michigan State University') seems to have a love-hate relationship with students, going on its PACE web page. This offers a guide to living in East Lansing, and includes:

66 **Sec. 302-4: Keep your lawn neat and trimmed. Grass should be no higher than six inches. [There is an $85 fine for long grass!]**

Sec. 302.10: Don't use or store indoor furniture on any porch, deck, balcony or lawn.

Sec. 302.11: Park in designated parking areas only. Don't drive or park on the lawn. 99

The most common argument advanced for making people keep neat lawns is that untidy lawns harbour weeds, and that provides a stock of seed that can invade other lawns. Just as mass vaccination benefits us all, say the lawn zealots, so proper lawn maintenance is good for all.

Surprisingly, the opposition to painfully ordered lawn dates back a lot further than we might think. In 1881, in *The Wild Garden*, William Robinson (1838–1935), wrote:

66 We want shaven carpets of grass here and there, but what nonsense it is to shave it as often as foolish men shave their faces! ... Who would not rather see the waving grass with countless flowers than a close surface without a blossom? Think of the labour wasted in this ridiculous work of cutting off the heads of flowers and grass. Let much of the grass grow till fit for hay. and we may enjoy in it a world of lovely flowers that will blossom and perfect their growth before hay time ... 99

Robinson was Irish-born, but he had settled in London, working at the botanical gardens at Regent's Park. He was writing at a time when most British gentlemen were still bearded, following a fashion that started when troops returned from the Crimean War, hence his reference to the 'foolish men' who shaved. In 1867, Charles Darwin (who by then wore a full beard) sponsored Robinson as a fellow of the Linnean Society. Robinson was influential, and wrote for both *The Gardener's Chronicle* and *The Times*, and influenced the British Arts and Crafts Movement.

I checked *The Wild Garden* and found no mention of lawn, or mowers or topiary, or even pests, other than rabbits. He was quite firm about those: 'there should be no rabbits in the wild garden', he said. Rabbits damaged trees, broke up the cover for pheasants and hares and so were a pest. His solution was interesting, given that less than 20 years earlier, convicted poachers were still being transported to Australia: invite some poachers into the garden! They would, he believed, probably even be willing to pay for the privilege.

What he really wanted was to see plants growing unfettered in natural settings, with self-sown plants able to prosper, but in the right way. In his view, a traditional garden with lawns and managed garden beds was fine near the house (hence his acceptance of 'shaven carpets of grass here and there'), but he urged the owners of larger properties to see the more distant portions as gardens of a particular sort. It did, at least, help to maintain a degree of biodiversity as plants were allowed to dictate their landscape, rather than leaving the decisions to a gardener or garden designer.

Where modern seekers after natural grassland are somewhat opposed to exotic plants in their environment, Robinson devoted two chapters to appropriate exotics—as he saw it: one of his approved species was the opium poppy! His gardens might resemble beards, but they would be beards with small ornaments dangling from them.

The Times also cited beards in the tidy garden matter, but two generations later. By then, hirsute pursuits were out of fashion, except among eccentric old men, and maybe a few naval personnel. One week after World War II ended, the paper was harrying its readers to get their gardens tidied up, now that peace allowed them some leisure. Mowing, argued a leader writer, is one of the arts of peace.

That said, the writer conceded that there might be those who resented the need to push a mower around on a sweltering afternoon, who saw the cessation of mowing as a small benefit of war. The writer chided them that the wild lawn which had erupted during the war was like a beard. Just as removing a beard was painful, so was taking off the overgrowth of weeds, 'but once it is done its owner rejoices in his new-found chin, and fondles its unaccustomed smoothness'.

Then the paper took out a small option on the alternative, a tiny concession that wilderness could also be beautiful. 'Thus it will doubtless be with the lawn, but before the mower gets to work and the dandelions fall, one last not ungrateful glance of farewell may be spared to that variegated wilderness'.

Some 15 years earlier, in June 1930, *The Times* had turned to the curious phenomenon of Hyde Park and its weeds—or its lack of them. Both Hyde Park and Green Park were almost lacking in weeds, unlike St James' Park. Part of the answer, said the reporter, was a large sterile band of urban paving, bricks and mortar, a *cordon sanitaire* where weeds were unable to flourish. This surrounded those parks and kept them safe from attack.

Another aspect was that the two weed-free parks each had three species of grass in their lawns, increasing the chance that there was a suitable species available to colonise any gap. With nothing but the cropping of sheep (which apparently were still there in both parks in 1930!) to reduce the grass, the combination of grasses was able to smother weeds.

Last of all, said the writer, London children probably played their part, plucking keenly at any flower which emerged, long before it could set seed. These theories leave out the effects of hay-eating horses, commonly encountered in the vicinity of St James' Park during ceremonial occasions. The effects of horses as a source of weed seed should not be discounted. For that matter, neither should the effects of unprocessed hay be left out of consideration, as Mr Froude noticed during his 1885 visit to Melbourne:

❝ The Observatory was but a quarter of a mile distant, but in the forenoon, and under a Victorian sun, we had a mauvais quart d'heure in getting there. On the way, amidst some coarse grass, I beheld a scarlet pimpernel, the veritable 'poor man's weatherglass' of

northern Europe, basking wide open in the rays. If I had been studying the language of the New Hebrides, and had found imbedded in it a Greek verb, perfect in all its inflexions, I could not have been more surprised. How in the wide world came a highly organised plant of this kind to be growing wild in Australia? Had the seed been brought by some ship's crew, or in a bird's stomach, or been wafted over in the chambers of the air? To what far-off connection did it point of Australia with the old world? I gathered my marvel, and carried it to Mr Ellery [the astronomer at the observatory] to be explained. How idly we let our imagination wander! He laughed as he said, 'Many weeds and wild flowers from the old country make their first appearance in this garden. Our instruments are sent out packed in hay'. **99**

Hay also carried many seeds to the Americas, some good, some bad. By 1647, a hay meadow had been sown with 'English grass', a mixture of white clover, fescues, bents, rye and bluegrasses. The seed had been sourced from chaff on immigrant ships, and by 1650, hayseed was being moved around the New England colonies, no doubt with seeds attached. Native Americans in New England and Virginia knew the plantain as 'Englishman's foot', from the way it followed European settlement.

But if laws demanding constant mowing will not defeat the weeds, there is another theory about these laws. Some critics say the Draconian rules in the USA about lawns helped to maintain an area's uniformity in terms of race and wealth. It helped to drive away, or at least to hide, any descent into what was seen as barbarism. The real targets, say these critics, were perceived human 'weeds', misfits, radicals and those of other cultures and races.

Still, the lawn rules motivated busy executives to give employment to indigent elements. Then again, maybe it is just a pursuit of outward perfection, where beds can be left unmade because they are hidden, but lawns are visible and so need to be tidy.

✵ ✵ ✵

DEFENDING THE LAWN

✳ ✳ ✳

Recovering a lawn after a catastrophic tree fall can take some hard work and cunning. I once had two shallow-rooted Eucalyptus trees come down in high winds. The roots came out of the ground, ripping up several square metres of lawn. By the time the trees had been removed and the stumps ground away, I was left with a large pile of woodchips and soil, which I needed to sieve and tamp down before planting with cuttings.

That was when I discovered the hidden enemies of lawn. The postman on his light motor-bicycle rode over the bare patch and neighbourhood children took it for a sandpit. Their priorities were more to finding places where they could play with model cars, but they clashed with my needs. I had done the hard work, now I used cunning to avoid confrontation.

I made a light fence with posts and string, and hung a sign 'DANGER: *Stenotaphrum* in enclosed area'. The postman began to avoid the area and walked to the letterbox, neighbours told their children not to play there, and only one childless couple asked me what *Stenotaphrum* was. 'It's buffalo grass', I said. They nodded and walked off, grinning. Blinding with science wins again!

My first day at an Australian university, I walked on a lawn and was advised by a member of the Students' Representative Council that one did not walk on the quadrangle lawn, save on the day one graduated. Other university grass and lawn was open slather, but not in the quad, she said.

Almost half a century on, I passed through the same quadrangle on the day I finished this book, and it seems that this stray European notion has now largely evaporated from Australian universities. Most people seem to keep to the paved areas when they pass through the quadrangle, but the 'keep off' signs have gone, and undergraduates may walk, sit and lie on the grass. We respect lawn, but we use it, because in a temperate climate, the grass recovers quickly.

There is a class of petty officialdom, however, that really enjoys enforcing restrictions. Jacob Riis was a journalist and photojournalist who liked to challenge authority. He left a lasting legacy, and even those who have never heard of him are likely to have heard the expression 'how the other half lives'. That phrase was the title of his 1890 account of tenement life in New York, in which the crusader used newly-invented flash bulbs to capture dismal interiors, to shake the complacency of the authorities.

By 1902, he was beginning to see some results, as he described in his later book, *The Battle with the Slum*. Thanks to his efforts Riis could offend by walking on the grass of a brand-new slum park:

> ❝ I had been out of town and my way had not fallen through the Mulberry Bend in weeks until that morning when I came suddenly upon the park that had been made there in my absence. Sod had been laid, and men were going over the lawn cutting the grass after the rain. The sun shone upon flowers and the tender leaves of young shrubs, and the smell of new-mown hay was in the air. Crowds of little Italian children shouted with delight over the 'garden,' while their elders sat around upon the benches with a look of contentment such as I had not seen before in that place. I stood and looked at it all, and a lump came in my throat as I thought of what it had

been, and of all the weary years of battling for this. It had been such a hard fight, and now at last it was won. To me the whole battle with the slum had summed itself up in the struggle with this dark spot. The whir of the lawn-mower was as sweet a song in my ear as that which the skylark sang when I was a boy, in Danish fields, and which gray hairs do not make the man forget.

'Keep off the grass!'

In my delight I walked upon the grass. It seemed as if I should never be satisfied till I had felt the sod under my feet,—sod in the Mulberry Bend! I did not see the gray-coated policeman hastening my way, nor the wide-eyed youngsters awaiting with shuddering delight the catastrophe that was coming, until I felt his cane laid smartly across my back and heard his angry command:

'Hey! Come off the grass! D'ye think it is made to walk on?'

So that was what I got for it. It is the way of the world. But it was all right. The park was there, that was the thing. And I had my revenge. I had just had a hand in marking five blocks of tenements for destruction to let in more light, and in driving the slum from two other strongholds. Where they were, parks are being made to-day in which the sign 'Keep off the grass!' will never be seen. The children may walk in them from morning till night, and I too, if I want to, with no policeman to drive us off. I tried to tell the policeman something about it. But he was of the old dispensation. All the answer I got was a gruff:

'G'wan now! I don't want none o' yer guff!' **"**

A bust of Vincent van Gogh taught me that other nations have other customs. When I was in France and saw the bust in a park in Arles, I was delighted. Now a quick low-brow briefing: those who know nothing of art and don't know what they like are likely to recall that poor Vincent cut his ear off.

In all probability, it was an accident that happened during an epileptic seizure, and should be a matter of sympathy. Sadly, the Australian larrikin, the cultural urchin within me spotted the potential dilemma that would have confronted the burghers of Arles. Either they had elected to pretend it never happened, so the bust would have both ears, or it would have an ear missing, in which case they were pandering to sensationalism.

Either way, I had to photograph it so I could share it with others of equal cultural shallowness. I saw that one ear was missing from the bust, and stepped onto the grass around the bust. As I did, I heard a stentorian roar from an enraged local guardian of public morals and parks. His French was indistinct but his gestures made it clear that he wanted me off the grass, but he was portly, elderly and somewhat distant. So I waved happily to him, took my picture, and was back on the path before he arrived.

I habitually walk gently on vegetation, but I realise now that the poor man probably had the challenging task of maintaining the grass around the bust. The thoughtless local powers-that-be had decided that it should be surrounded by vulnerable lawn. It was they who selected a weak and easily trampled grass when they ought to have chosen the more robust species of temperate climes—or gravel—to surround One-ear Vince. Perhaps they thought it was a nice lush colour.

THE ART OF THE LAWNSMAN

Making a lawn demands a lawn maker with enough sense to choose the right grass. Lawns are unnatural, and never emerge in the wild. You may see meadows that look at a distance like lawn, you may see small cropped patches that look like lawn, but broad expanses offer too many gaps where animals, plants and small living things can intervene and feed. Grass survives, lawn does not. One thing that never goes astray in a lawn maker is a measure of insanity, but the main thing is choosing the right grass species and strain or variety.

For clarity, it is better to use scientific names in any discussion on grasses, because common names have a habit of changing from place to place. It happens even with trees: the Australian mountain ash is the tallest flowering plant, *Eucalyptus regnans*, but in Texas, a mountain ash is *Fraxinus texensis* while the rest of North America uses the same name to refer to the genus *Sorbus*. In Britain, the mountain ash is a single species, the rowan, *Sorbus aucuparia*.

Still, there is a romance in the common names like Yorkshire fog (*Holcus lanatus*), hairy panic (*Panicum effusum*)—also called arse grass, because if you stand still, you will be up to that part in it, five minute grass (*Tripogon loliiformis*), neat lovegrass (*Eragrostis basedowii*), neverfail grass (*Eragrostis setifolia*), winter grass or annual bluegrass (*Poa annua*), crabgrass (*Digitaria sanguinalis*), devil's grass or Bermuda or Bahamas grass, (*Cynodon dactylon*), itchgrass (*Rottboellia exaltata*), stink grass (*Eragrostis cilianensis*), not to mention less lawn-like grasses such as wiregrass, firegrass, knotty butt grass, rat's tail couch, spike grass, spring grass and sweet grass.

Like most people who contribute to the web, I try to use the formal 'scientific names' on my pages because those names mean one thing only. On the principle that readers here may wish to take a matter further, I have opted to provide the formal names here at least once for important grasses. I confess that I wavered on this, but even if Latin precision is potentially alarming, at least it is more precise and informative to the lawnsman than 'black beetles will eat itch grass'.

The discerning reader may have seen by now that this is not a lawnsman's manual, but I imagine that my readers will include lawnsmen with curious minds. I shall not apologise again for the gender specificity of my terms: I submit that the vast majority of women are far too sensible to become enmeshed in the torrid and wearying arts of lawn maintenance. I am aware of a Memphis Tennessee firm which sends bikini-clad young females out to mow the lawns of gentlemen, and I deal elsewhere with that and with women 'mowers' as depicted in lawn mower ads, but this is all fantasy stuff. So without intending any offence, I will stand by my terminology.

Precision in defining a species is not enough for the dedicated lawnsman. As with other species that have been grown and selected (or indeed with wild species), a grass that is suited to lawns comes in many variant forms.

When these have been developed artificially, they are cultivars like breeds of dog. Each has been shaped by horticulturists to the needs of the industry, using all that we know of genetics. The density, colour, texture and resistance of each strain to drought and disease has been measured and heightened.

Remember the grass that made silica bits when the voles chewed it? There was a cost associated with doing that, which is why the grass stopped making silica when the voles stopped chewing. Almost everything in life is a trade-off, and that applies to grass cultivars. Merion Kentucky bluegrass was thought excellent on baseball fields in the 1950s because it is deep-rooted (which helped it grow back from scuffing) and it has a great colour, but sooner or later, a pest will show up which can exploit that.

I cannot stress enough that grass is not lawn. To achieve a lawn, one needs suitable grass seed or turf, a fair amount of work, a great deal of money, incredible patience and a capacity for infinite vigilance. The main thing is work, and that brings us to the excellent Mr Beale, who published *The Book of the Lawn* in 1931. Reginald Beale was a Fellow of the Linnean Society and also both a director and the Manager, Sports and Grass Department at Carter's Tested Seeds Ltd. He committed his life to lawn, and took a no-prisoners approach to the making of it.

Preparation required the surface to be dug-over to spade-length, turning the soil to the depth of the blade of the spade, while working in 'one load of well-rotted dung, stable litter or peat moss per hundred square yards'. Then the surface had to be trod down, rolled and raked to firmness. If the surface needed levelling, the uppermost six inches of topsoil had to be set aside so the subsoil may be worked to a level, before the topsoil was replaced and spread evenly.

In Beale's view, a garden lawn could range from a few square yards to a couple of acres, but in each case, it demanded the same treatment, though clearly he preferred the larger size. His own lawn was 2000 square yards, not far short of half an acre, and it included a putting course of 500 square yards. Perhaps the reader wanted to set down a regulation bowling green: this would be 42 yards on a side, 1764 square yards.

Lawn makers had developed some tricks of the trade by the end of the 1870s, little rules of thumb that achieved the desired effect. Some of them look questionable today, like the advice to never reduce a lawn to a perfect level.

ASIDE from repair situations, Antipodeans find admonitions to keep off the grass quaint and foreign. It properly belongs to class-riddled and effete northern nations, who use the privilege of grass walking as a way of separating the sheep from the goats. In many societies, particularly in cooler northern regions where grass struggles, lawn is venerated and defended, and only the grand may walk over it.

The middle of the lawn, the experts said, should be raised by two feet in the centre, so as to avoid the centre 'appearing hollow'.

Mr Beale would have been shocked at that rule, because his lawns not only had to look good, they had to provide a true playing surface. There might be a slight slope to allow drainage, though his book, like a number of works after about 1880, recommends sub-surface drainage to remove excess water and features plans for this sort of work.

The holy grail of lawn breeders is to find or breed a single grass that will flourish in all climates, under all attacks and under all regimes, but this is close to an impossible dream. The alternative is (or has been in the past) to send out adventurers who will find and bring back samples of grass to be tested, inspected, dissected, reflected upon and then tested some more. After that, the new finds can be sold, either as seed or as rolls of turf.

Seeds were used to transfer grass species from continent to continent, mainly because seeds were so much easier to keep alive. *Cynodon dactylon* is known in the USA as Bermuda (or Bahamas) grass, though it actually originated in Africa, and was taken to America as a pasture plant. The same species is called 'couch' in Australia, which acquired it from India. *Poa pratensis* is known to Americans as Kentucky bluegrass, but it is not a native.

The parentage of Kentucky bluegrass is open to debate or even dispute. It may have been introduced from Britain, or France or Germany, depending on the authority you believe. Some recent research, however, points to the grass having spread from Labrador or Alaska, but there may have been multiple introductions (including the early 'English grass' meadows). We will never know for certain.

One decidedly non-lawn grass, sugar cane, was taken to the New World by Columbus in 1493, and on the Spanish Main, local people were so taken with this crop that it travelled even faster than Spanish influence, so the conquistadores kept seeing sugar cane in virgin territory, and thought it must be native to the area. Some of them even wondered if the Indians might have brought it by canoe from the Philippines! The moral is that we need to be careful with our inferences about origins.

Sometimes, the common name is a good indication of the general source. Kikuyu grass, *Pennisetum clandestinum*, beloved of Australian golf course keepers and loathed by Australian gardeners for its invasive style, was brought to Australia from southern Africa. In some parts of Australia, it is now regarded as a noxious weed, and it had to be controlled on Montague Island off the Australian coast because it grew so thickly that penguins could not reach their nests. Not all grass is good grass!

An early colonial governor, Henry Ellis, is sometimes credited with taking Bermuda grass to Savannah, Georgia, though it may have been an accidental import from Africa, perhaps in slave ships. Johnsongrass (*Sorghum halepense*) was deliberately introduced into South Carolina from Turkey in 1830, and by 1840, it had reached Alabama. Along the way, it changed, possibly by forming a hybrid with a different local *Sorghum* species.

Paspalum notatum, known to Australians just as paspalum, is Bahia grass in the USA, but its origins lie in central and South America. Just out of curiosity, I pursued this grass through some other languages. Other English names include forquilha grass, notatum grass, and Paraguay paspalum. It is *herbe de Bahia* in French, *forquilha* in Brazil, *bahia* (among other names) in Spanish, but *pasto bahia* in Colombia and Mexico, *grama* in El Salvador, *ya-bahia* in Thailand, *co san dâú* in Vietnam and *rumput pencasilan* in Indonesia.

There is probably a whole history of grass transfers buried in those names, but few grass romances can match the tale of Frank N Meyer (1875–1918), a Dutch-American agricultural explorer. Born in Amsterdam, he worked in Asia, collecting plants and seeds of many species.

He began his working life in the Amsterdam Botanical Gardens, then after walking around Europe, moved to England and then the USA in 1901, where he worked first in the greenhouses along the Mall in Washington DC before heading to California, Mexico and Missouri. His next target was the Andes, but he was persuaded to go to China instead.

His biographer, Isabel Shipley Cunningham, says that he sent back many seeds, but also cuttings, packed in damp *Sphagnum* moss, oil cloth and then stitched into burlap (hessian cloth). It was a delicate balance to make the moss just dry enough not to rot the cuttings and just damp enough to allow live material to survive the long journey back to the USA. Lest we picture his trip as idyllic, Cunningham describes how Meyer slept in filthy inns with brick beds, where bedbugs, lice, scorpions and centipedes were his companions, but there was worse:

> **"** At dusk he would watch the sun setting over the ice fields of the Amur, silhouetting the white birches against the dying purple of the sky. One evening, as he returned to his inn, three murderous ruffians attacked him, but he drew his bowie knife and defended himself so vigorously that they ran away. **"**

It should come as little surprise to us that Meyer died mysteriously in 1918 when he drowned after going overboard from a ship on the Yangtze River. He had been ill and may have fallen, he might have committed suicide, but there were those who preferred to hint darkly that he was murdered by being thrown overboard. The case, if there was one, was never solved.

What we do know is that he has a lasting memorial, or several, if you count some of the larger plants he collected, some of which are still alive). His best known memorial is a grass, Meyer *Zoysia*, which was released in 1951. The genus *Zoysia* includes a number of creeping grasses that make an elegant coating over any surface. The genus was once only found in Asia and its name commemorates Karl von Zoys zu Laubach (1756-1800). He was a Slovenian botanist and plant collector, but back then, as he was in the Austrian empire, the Austrians called him 'von Zois', which causes lots of confusion because of the spelling change. The plant was actually named by Carl Ludwig Willdenow (1765-1812), in 1801, but there seems to be no indication of whether he was commemorating the recently-deceased collector. Given the timing, he probably was making a memorial.

In parts of Asia, it was common to place sods of *Zoysia* on freshly closed graves, and mourners used to go out to collect these in the wild, which meant that Meyer could get a wide range of samples by what one assumes was a fairly surreptitious robbing of old graves. The Meyer *Zoysia* was a strain of *Zoysia japonica* released by the US Department of Agriculture and the US Golf Association Green Section, after a breeding program that started with material grown from seed in 1940.

Seed was the common way of moving new grasses between continents in the nineteenth century, and grass seed is commonly used in establishing lawns today. Until well into the twentieth century there was no retail trade in grass seed. In 1784, the D Landreth Seed Company was established in Philadelphia.

In 1863, an anonymous scribe wrote them up in *The Atlantic Monthly* in a piece called 'American Horticulture'. By then, Bloomsdale was the centre of the company's operations, and the writer called it 'the most prominent and widest-known of seed farms', but no grass seeds were mentioned.

Arriving at the front, visitors would find themselves 'in the midst of a lawn of ten acres in the English style' (meaning like a park). There was wide variety, and the seeds listed as being available from Bloomsdale's 400 acres include turnip, cabbage, radish, beet and lettuce in many varieties. Yet among these gardens, designed to yield commercial quantities of seed, there were no facilities for the production of grass seeds. In 1863, there was no market for grass seed.

One thing is certain: if you lay turf, you have an almost instant lawn, while a new lawn that is grown from seed will take much of the growing season to come into its own, but laying turf is something of an art, and most of us will be coerced into calling in a specialist.

My first experience of the greenkeeper's art came when we decided to replace an unsightly lawn with a shade and drought-resistant form of *Stenotaphrum* (buffalo grass) after a chance meeting over dinner with a greenkeeper turned turf consultant. Half-measures were never going to be brought into play, and in early March, as a southern autumn advanced, two men turned up with sprays to poison the grass, the weeds and everything else.

It was quick, and it was deadly. It was so quick that the first any of the neighbours knew was when the grass, over a couple of days went from a chlorotic yellow-green to a dull brown as the leaves withered and gasped their last. Neighbours walked past and looked askance at the ugly mess that was our yard and street lawn. Unlike most Australian homes, we had an American-style lawn that progressed from our property to the nature strip, the public portion, without an intervening fence. We asked the poisoners to kill and replace that as well, so the whole area looked devastated.

Then on March 16, a truck rolled into the street, and neatly-packed rolls of turf were stacked on the verge by an ugly and profoundly squat but highly efficient folding forklift. Close behind came our greenkeeper and his assistants, who spread the rolls out over the top of the dead grass before thrusting a manual into my hands and issuing stern advice about watering and not walking on the grass before they departed.

We were left to look at our beautiful instant lawn. The date of delivery, March 16, would stick in our minds afterwards, because a neighbour came past, a few minutes later, as we wrestled the soaker hose, the special sprinkler and other items into place. He was one of those who had been casting dubious eyes over the tragic browns, and now he admired the expanse of green.

'Hmmm! Got a special dye job for St Patrick's Day, did you? Not bad!'

When Lewis Carroll described gardeners painting white roses red in chapter 7 of *Alice's Adventures in Wonderland*, he was writing a calculated nonsense, but what are we to make of Winterlawn, a grass dye widely sold in the US right through the 1950s and used to colour golf courses, sports fields, and cemeteries? This artfully concealed disease spots and the brown patches left by dormant winter grasses, and the practice continues. As I was drafting this chapter, I heard that grass in the major streets of Beijing was treated with 'Ever Green' brand greening liquid, imported from the US, just for the Olympics.

It is probably no worse (and probably less harmful to the environment) than the modern-day use of water to achieve the same effect in grass-unfriendly places like Phoenix, Arizona. Indeed, the Chinese authorities claimed that the liquid had 'been given a green light by the US Environment Protection Center (sic),' according to Jiang Xiaoyu, vice-president of the Beijing 2008 Olympic Games Bidding Committee. Dyes, however, were not the only things sprayed, spread or painted on lawns, because green grass has many enemies.

FIGHTING PESTS

The simple principle of the idealised suburban lawn was an expanse of a single species, a monoculture, a delicious meal, sprawling there, inviting fungi, bacteria, slime moulds, insects, worms and all manner of vertebrates to come and dine, above or below ground. To a biologist, creating a monoculture is not just standing in front of the bulls at Pamplona, it is charging the bulls, waving a flag and blowing a trumpet. It is either terminally muddle-headed or determinedly suicidal.

So if you were writing a recipe for an urban ecological disaster, you could not do worse than to start with a lawn, but people did. So they needed to use toxins, fearful treatments that only served to reduce the problem or to make it go next door, ready to emerge again, as soon as the spraying stopped.

Then there is the evolutionary law of large numbers: if an almost infinite number of small life forms is trying to eat your lawn, even if it has been specially bred for resistance, sooner or later, a strain of pest will arise by chance which can eat or attack that grass variant. With none of its fellows able to live there, it will thrive and reproduce. Before long, the breeder's careful work will avail us nought.

The solution may lie with biological controls. These are organisms which prey on pests, hopefully infecting others before they kill their host. If your lawn is attacked by rabbits, perhaps myxomatosis or calicivirus would do the trick, if only you could source some. (This may be harder than you think, and then the next challenge is to introduce the disease to the targets, and if conditions are not right for the mosquitoes, fleas or other animals that spread the disease, you may have problems.)

A more useful biological control for some lawn pests is a dose of predatory nematodes (or eelworms) which chew their way into a host (usually a larva of some sort). These are less than a millimetre long, too small to see. All the same, the right nematodes can be deadly to pests. They introduce bacteria which kill the host, and the nematode lays eggs. These later become adult nematodes which pick up some bacterial spores before they leave their 'nest' to find targets of their own, and so it goes.

Nematodes are versatile beasts, and between them, they will attack almost anything, so you need to get the right one, something like *Heterorhabditis zelandica*, which professionals spray on turf to control curl grubs. Choose the wrong nematode, and nearby strawberries, onions, potatoes or peas may suddenly keel over, or at least get very sick! The average nematode does more good than harm, releasing nitrogen compounds back into the soil, and with luck, we will hear more about *good* nematodes in the future!

When I was, many moons ago, a teacher of biology, I would set my students the thought-experiment of coming up with a plan to breed snails which preferentially ate onion-weed. Most biological controls are naturally there and just need to be let loose, but my young thinkers learned a bit about the need for large numbers in evolution through that exercise. Along the way, we also needed to look at what it meant to be a weed.

Weeds are defined in operational terms: any plant which grows where it is not wanted is a weed. Sometimes, though, people have mixed feelings about weeds. The Brazilian *Lantana* that is currently contained by biological controls in Australia is a pest plant, yet it gives small songbirds a place to nest where feral cats cannot go.

The dandelion was introduced to Australia as a medicinal plant, yet it is seen as a weed in lawns, when it invades them. Most weeds are opportunist invaders. In nature, weeds grow in disturbed places. That means they show up where an animal has been digging, where a tree has fallen over, with its roots ripping out of the ground, or perhaps where there has been a fire.

A freshly-dug garden bed and a freshly-sown lawn both appear to weeds as ideal disturbed habitats. So does the place where you have dug up (or poisoned) an existing weed. The other thing successful weeds have going for them is that they produce huge numbers of seeds, even if only a few of them will survive. Crab-grass (or summer-grass) can produce up to a million seeds in a square yard or square metre.

Sometimes, we seem to go out of our way to make things right for weeds. Mowing the lawn makes an artificial environment, and if some grasses can survive there, that does not mean they prosper. Crab-grass, on the other hand, gains from mowing. For example, a crab-grass seed needs a short burst of direct sunlight if it is to germinate, and mowing a lawn lets the sunlight reach the seeds. Dig over a garden or set the blades too low, and the crab-grass will emerge. Let there be rain after a dry spell, and out comes the crab-grass, as if by magic. Small wonder, then, that lawn lovers will resort to 'magic' sprays which promise to wage war on the evil weeds!

�֎ ✷ ✷

CHEMICAL WARFARE

Weeds are inevitable: if they did not exist, they would emerge. If the soil is not treated before seeding, weeds emerge with the grass. If they don't check the material on sale, careless buyers can end up stuck with weedy turf. Lawn lovers are told that a few weeds in the sod may be acceptable, since they may be extracted during the laying. The alternative to hand-culling is spraying, but that can bring its own problems.

7

❝ The first 2,4-D ever applied to a lawn for selective weed control was sprayed onto my lawn in the summer of 1943. Columbus discovering America hardly had more of a thrill than I had as I saw the leaves of tough old Dandelions twist and curl as they writhed in death agony. ❞

R. Milton Carleton, *The New Way to Kill Weeds in Your Lawn and Garden.*

A quarter-century after Carleton tested 2,4-D, as US aircraft were using Agent Orange (which included 2,4-D) on the jungles of Vietnam, retail sellers of pesticides (and I was one of them) reassured the public that those same chemicals could safely be used on lawns, where they would defoliate only the weeds. The principle was quite clear: 'broad-leaved' plants or dicotyledons were more easily killed by certain sprays like 2,4-D than were the grasses. In the language of the garden chemicals industry, it was a 'selective' weedkiller.

The components of Agent Orange probably had significant amounts of impurities in the form of a nasty group of poisons, the dioxins. Some scientists even thought for a while that it may have been the dioxins which poisoned the plants. Ignorant of that, we retailers parroted that 2,4-D was a plant hormone, that would only kill weeds. It was safe around people, we said, and to clinch our expertise, we would refer to it as '2,4 dichlorophenoxyacetic acid', and the punters would look impressed at our verbal skills and hand over their

money. There is more than one way of blinding with science, but the public was willing to believe, because above all, the public hated lawn pests.

Reginald Beale hated all pests, but 2,4-D would have disappointed him, because his aim, first and foremost, was to slay earthworms, and 2,4-D makes little difference to their populations. Whatever the work, said Beale in *The Book of the Lawn*, worms needed to be killed. He showed a missionary zeal in encouraging others to fall upon their earthworms and slay them. The best product that he could recommend, was his own company's 'Carter's worm killer', invented in 1902.

> **"** It is hopeless to renovate turf that is full of worms, because they will simply push the young plants out of the ground or smother them with their casts, so before starting work they must be killed. **"**

To bring the baseline of a tennis court up to his standards, his first step was to kill the worms, which he said would otherwise smother the young plants with their casts. True, he worked for Carter's Seeds, a big influence in the lawn business, but he sincerely believed in total war on worms:

> **" Worms.—Of the few pests that attack Turf in this country the earthworm takes the premier position and undoubtedly does more harm than all the rest together**

... their slimy casts make wonderful seed-beds for weeds, and in consequence they are always found together, and more or less in ratio.

The more one studies the subject the more apparent it becomes that where they abound, the turf is not only coarse, weedy, tender, soft, muddy, and wears out quickly; but where they are conspicuous by their absence it is finer in quality, freer from weeds, firmer and cleaner underfoot, much stronger, and can be kept clean and bright with a true, accurate surface all the year round. 99

Destroying worms required guile. First, the lawnsman had to leave his lawn unrolled, to encourage the worms to open up their runs or tunnels. This was the calm before the storm, the day before Armageddon, the moment when the forces of the righteous were poised to swarm over the plague of evil worms and smite them.

Having waited patiently, the English lawnsman must wait for a dull, misty, muggy warm day, with the wind in the south or the west, so the worms would be active. Even so, it was necessary to make a test. One pound of worm killer was to be laid down on two square yards of lawn and watered in, a dosage equal to 270 grams per square metre. Then the lawnsman waited and watched the selected patch.

If, said Beale, '... worms, large and small, struggle to the surface in thousands to die', then conditions are right, and the rest of the lawn may be treated at the same level of half a pound per square yard'. There seems to be no record of the active ingredient, but the dosage adds up to more than a ton of worm killer powder to an acre, or 2.4 tons per hectare!

Beale assured his readers that his company's wormkiller was infallible on the right day, but if the worms did not emerge in thousands, the lawnsman should wait for another day. There were two stages in the test, he said: the first worm should appear on the surface and die in about 15 minutes, and by 30 minutes, there should be a hundred or more dead worms in the test plot. Once the lawn was treated, the lawnsman should look out for the occasional invading worm and kill it by hand.

We don't know what was in Carter's wormkiller, but most of the poisons before World War II were based on heavy metals (lead, arsenic and the like) or toxic organic compounds, and these were splashed around with a happy lack of care or concern. If the wormkiller contained heavy metals, there was probably an inert dilutant, going on the dosage that Beale recommended.

His concern over worms may seem a little odd to us today, even if it was quite normal for a lawn lover in that era. The role of earthworms in aerating the soil and dragging vegetation down into the soil to provide humus is well known and understood, but not everybody thinks their presence is a plus. In *Your Lawn*, Milton Carleton dismisses the views of 'earthworm fans' as poppycock, arguing that earthworms 'will only live in rich soil, and if it is really rich they cannot contribute anything to it'.

Carleton shows his biological credentials on the next page where he writes 'One of the most damaging lawn insects is not an insect but a stage—the grub—of a variety of beetles …'. Still, he is right in raising the link between moles and worms, because moles eat earthworms. If worm casts on a lawn are bad, molehills must be Evil Incarnate.

THE NON-WORM PESTS

Terrestrial moles are mammals with poor sight and a deficient sense of smell, but with heightened powers to feel and hear. They dig deep burrows, dumping soil on the surface to make molehills, and they also make surface runs which they use to find food. These runs can damage turf roots in established lawns, or kill plants in newly seeded plots.

Beale claimed that a one-foot length of lit miners' safety fuse, placed in a mole run, would gas the villains. He mused that perhaps smoky fireworks would also do the job. Sadly, there is little sense in trying to smoke or gas moles, because most of the fumes just disperse through the soil. That aside, moles are smart enough to block off any section of a run or burrow that has dangerous smells coming through it.

In 1932, a correspondent complained in *The Times* about birds pecking holes in his lawn, prompting a reply from Nathaniel Lloyd, Chairman of the Green Committee at Rye Golf Club. He suggested that the birds were probably catching the larvae of tipulid flies, commonly known as daddy longlegs or crane flies. The solution was to kill the larvae, commonly known as leather-jackets. Dilute carbolic acid, he said, would bring them to the surface, where they might be swept away, before they could recover and burrow in again.

He added that other recommended remedies included paris green, nicotine and carbon disulfide, but he dismissed them all. Beale had recommended carbon disulfide, though, saying that it was also good against ants (which he also hated). He did warn that it is somewhat dangerous because it is inflammable. He could have added that it is also explosive, absorbed through the skin (which it burns), and toxic in higher doses.

The best treatment for leather-jackets, Lloyd believed, was lead arsenate at the rate of 5 pounds per thousand square feet. This amounts to about 24 grams (an amount large enough to kill a small adult) on each square metre (or square yard). He did have the grace to caution that this might be a danger to sheep, although he added brightly that lead arsenate 'does not appear to affect birds'.

By comparison, in 1957, Milton Carleton proposed using 10 or even 15 pounds of lead arsenate per 1000 square feet. While repeated treatments might build up lead and arsenic levels and damage grass, one dose would serve to rid the lawn of all the insect pests which also attracted moles. There was a better way, though, said Carleton: use Chlordane, which was as effective as 50 times its weight of lead arsenate.

Pearlwort (*Sagina procumbens*), an invasive weed that looks somewhat like moss may be eradicated by applying four ounces per square yard of a mix of 'three parts sulphate of ammonia, one part sulphate of iron, 20 parts sand', according to Henry Woodhead, who reported to *The Times* that he had found this recipe in 'a valuable Ministry of Agriculture pamphlet, printed in 1931'.

Woodhead was writing six months after Lloyd. Curiously, his level of application of the chemical component was of the order of 5 pounds per 1000 square feet, the same level Lloyd proposed for lead arsenate, though it would surely have been far less toxic.

The insecticide DDT was first synthesised in 1874, but it was only in 1939 that a chemist named Paul Müller saw how useful it was for killing insects. No human fatalities have ever been recorded from DDT, so the toxic dose of DDT in humans, if there is one must be greater than 10 milligrams per kilogram of body weight. In one study, human volunteers took 35 milligrams per day for a year, with no apparent harm. Nobody knows to this day how it kills insects, but one theory is that it probably acts on insect nerves.

DDT, THE WONDER COMPOUND

Historically, disease has generally been the greatest wartime killer of humans, what with disruption to supplies and groups of people being forced into close contact. In particular, diseases that may be spread by insects can flourish in the chaos that surrounds any modern war.

DDT was tested in 1942 and then used to control mosquitoes that might spread malaria. It was also used to stop a typhus outbreak among refugees in Naples, where around 1.3 million people were dusted with the white powder at the rate of 10 pounds to 150 people. This destroyed the lice that spread typhus and the outbreak stopped in its tracks. No humans showed signs of harm, and DDT was greeted as a new marvel.

Winston Churchill praised the insecticide in September 1944, saying 'The excellent DDT powder, which has been fully experimented with and found to yield astonishing results, will henceforth be used on a great scale by the British forces in Burma and by the American and Australian forces in the Pacific and India in all theatres'.

So DDT, identified as having never been shown to harm humans, was admired as a miracle white powder that did for our (non-human) enemies. At the war's end, soldiers returned home to Britain, the US and Australia, knowing from their experience with DDT, that sprays could be very effective. They were filled with the hubris of victory, and determined to win on the home front against the insect enemies that robbed them of their perfect lawn.

In fact, part of the campaign began in 1944, or even earlier, as advertisers were less than subtle in equating the insect enemies and the human enemies. In 1944, *Life* magazine offered this opinion about a common turf pest: 'Japanese beetles, unlike the Japanese, are without guile. There are, however, many parallels between the two. Both are small but very numerous and prolific, as well as voracious, greedy, and devouring'.

Following the same jingoistic and racist line, at the end of the war, DDT was seen as a domestic version of the atom bomb, able to deliver a quick knock-out against the enemy in the garden, the back yard and the front yard.

You have to wonder a little what the scientists were thinking and doing. As far back as Charles Darwin, who wrote a whole book on earthworms, naturalists had sung the praises of these admittedly slimy animals, and by the 1940s, people understood enough of Darwin's principle of selection. They must have known that the end result of tossing poisons around would be the evolution of resistant strains.

Within a year of Fleming, Chain and Florey receiving their Nobel Prize for penicillin in 1945, the first cases of penicillin-resistant bacteria had been observed, and by 1947, the medical journals carried a number of detailed reports, so the rise of DDT-resistance should have been anticipated, but like a navy faced with stronger armour plate on the other side, the sprayers just increased their firepower by raising the dosage.

In time, sanity emerged when people like Rachel Carson spoke out. Her book *The Silent Spring* was significant in raising public awareness of the wider effects of spraying, beyond the sprayed area. To do this, she looked at both the effects and the dosages. 'Users of one product, for example, apply sixty pounds of technical chlordane per acre if they follow directions,' she said. On rough figures, that would be enough to kill about 1200 large-ish humans, or rather more smaller mammals.

Carson showed how the use of chemical sprays like 2,4-D to control broad-leaved weeds actually opens up spaces where crab-grass seed can gain a hold; another product she mentioned delivered 175 pounds of arsenic per acre. She asked darkly how lethal these lawns may be for human beings. Once again, in ballpark figures, a dedicated poisoner using controlled and measured doses could probably kill 50,000 humans with that much arsenic.

In reality, far smaller and more carefully regulated doses can kill just as easily. In 1982, a US Navy Lieutenant named George Prior, died after he played 36 holes of golf at the Army-Navy Country Club in Arlington. He was 30, and apparently healthy, but he complained of a headache during the last hole.

That night, he developed a fever and nausea, and developed a rash. Within four days, he was running a temperature of 104.5°F (40.3°C), and his body was covered with blisters. After two weeks, the skin had gone from 80%

of his body, and he died after his major organs failed. Later investigations showed that he had been poisoned by Daconil 2787, an approved fungicide which had been sprayed on the course, twice a week.

Prior was most probably hypersensitive to the fungicide. The main problem, though, was that he generally carried his golf tee in his mouth, and this is probably how the poison got into his body. His widow later sued the manufacturer for US$20 million; the case was settled out of court so the terms of settlement remain unknown.

THE BATTLE OF THE DUCKS

In November 2007, golfers at one public course in Sydney, Australia, had had enough. Native wood ducks were being attracted to the greens of Warringah Golf Club. Once there, they dug up the greens, foraging for food, and they left little piles of what the club's general manager politely called faeces, all over the greens. The club had tried placing 'cat-like objects' and 'moving objects' near the greens to deter the ducks, which became used to the deterrents and returned.

The desperate golfers demanded action, so the club hired a shooter, who was instructed to use a silencer, to avoid distressing possible witnesses, but when shooting started, the grass-preservation imperative of the golfers was confronted by the animal-protection imperative of animal-lovers. Greens were dug up in the night, and a stern message left on cardboard: 'WARNING: you bastards kill one bird and we will destroy all your greens at our leisure. We will be watching and waiting'.

The club declared itself outraged by this 'vigilante behaviour'. They pointed out that the ducks were not a protected species, and that the club was licensed to act as it did. A National Parks and Wildlife spokesman explained that the hope was to discourage the birds: 'Normally, if they get rid of a few the other ducks get the message'.

All the same, Carson or not, vigilantes or not, strong action has been the order of the day for most lawnsmen alive today, but they direct their strong action against pests. Unfortunately, there was a price to pay. The microarthropods, the tiny animals that broke down leaf litter and lawn clippings, are also affected by the sprays. The soil, the leaf litter and compost heaps are all full of nematodes springtails, mites and other living things, smaller than a full stop.

Probably the only time gardeners see these is when a flower-pot is lifted when the weather is wet. Then, perhaps, tiny white dots may be seen, jumping up and down—these are springtails, and around them, there will be mites and other wriggly things, maybe even some pseudoscorpions that you can see if you put some of the leaf litter and dirt on a white plate or a sheet of white paper. These tiny animals live in a world of their own, eating vegetable matter or micro-organisms and fungi that 'eat' the vegetable matter, or eating each other.

Start spraying, and the delicate balance breaks down. The lawn clippings from a sprayed lawn have to be disposed of as waste, meaning the keen lawnsman must add more fertiliser, and so on. The lawn lovers who spray have stepped onto a treadmill that offers no escape.

There is a distinction to be made between a grassy expanse that one may look over with warm feelings on the one hand, and the perfect and unblemished surface that is demanded for the playing of bowls or the putting of balls on the other. With due respect, the croquet player of backbone will relish a surface with flaws, snares and delusions in the surface, seeing them with delight as contributors to the greater bloodiness of the game.

Those kindly souls who see croquet as a genteel activity undertaken on the vicarage lawn at tea parties have only played *at* croquet, they have never played croquet which combines fiendish cunning, a devilish eye, and an impish, almost caddish lack of respect and regard for the finer feelings of one's opponents, but that is a matter we will look into later. Croquet played by experts is like the lawnsman's pursuit of pests, unremitting and unforgiving warfare without any hint of chivalry or diplomacy.

To the proud lawn owner, an outbreak of moss indicates a serious weakness and the literature is full of warnings that it will 'take over'. Iron (II) or ferrous sulfate is usually indicated, though chlorophen (2,3,4,5,6-pentachlorophenol) can be used. Surely, this is an example of spraying gone mad, using poisons on a problem that ought to be dealt with on Darwinian principles? If it can handle the weeding, walking and watering regime of the lawn, then let it be! After all, if you have a bare patch in shade, what else can you do? Astroturf it?

When the ground is bare soil, the would be lawn-owner is tempted to welcome, cheer and coddle every sprig of greenness. In newly sown seed lawns, all vegetation is greeted as an advance; lawn becomes an elastic term, open to a degree of judicious leniency. The experienced lawnsman knows better than to be kind.

In time, the dedicated and competitive lawn lover must set aside all thoughts of tolerance, and it is then that the lawn lover recognises how much better it would have been to engage in ruthless extirpation from the very beginning.

It is the nature of the weed to be an opportunist: weeds produce many, many seeds that drift here and there, looking for disturbed ground where they may take brief root, producing seeds before pushing on—or spreading out. If you want a weedless expanse, never give a sucker or weedlet an even break.

You can tell how serious lawn people feel about weeds when a Peanuts character can observe that 'Big sisters are the crabgrass in the lawn of life', or when P.J. O'Rourke can observe that:

" The Democrats are the party that says government will make you smarter, taller, richer, and remove the crabgrass on your lawn. The Republicans are the party that says government doesn't work and then they get elected and prove it. "

Crabgrass (in the USA), known as summer grass in Australia, is one of those straggly banes of the gardener and lawnsman. Nobody, surely, could ever love crabgrass? This main target is *Digitaria sanguinalis* (which my vestigial Latin translates as something not unlike 'bloody fingers'), but that is just one of 300 species of *Digitaria*. None of them is particularly lovable, but crabgrass can limit erosion, a few *Digitaria* species are useful as pasture, and Australians use *Digitaria didactyla* as a lawn grass, calling it Queensland blue couch.

Some grasses like rye-grass and *Paspalum* can be infected by different species of a fungal group known as ergot, some of them even by the fearfully dangerous ergot, *Claviceps purpurea*, which produces powerful toxic and hallucinogenic chemicals—the popular 1960s drug, LSD, is an ergot derivative. Some people take the view that ergot has been a major killer in the past.

MOLES are generally small—weigh about 85 grams (3 ounces), and measure 15 cm (6 inches)—but they wreak tremendous havoc as they add two body lengths to a surface run in one minute. Sufferers are left with a few choices: poison, camphor balls, planting caper spurge and flooding the holes are all mentioned as possibilities, but trapping is the only method that really works. It is that or go for a more natural lawn, a kicked-about knockabout lawn where pleasure and nature come first, and moles are tolerated.

Ergot attacks rye, and if the fruiting bodies end up in bread, madness and mayhem follow: the burned witches of Salem may even have been victims of ergotomania. Luckily, we need to swallow the ergot for any ill effects to emerge, so as long as you mow your grass and don't eat the clippings, you ought to be OK!

Lawn grasses do, however, suffer from a few other fungal attacks, mainly cereal rusts. While the lawn manuals will offer all sorts of ideas for sprays, watering the grass less will usually solve the problem for your lawn.

LAWN PESTS FOR FUN AND AMUSEMENT

One amusing 'pest-that-isn't' is the group of organisms known as slime moulds. For some time, these were treated as a peculiar fungus, and so mycologists, fungal specialists, got to work with them. When the slime moulds get on your roses or lawn, they make a neat mildew-like coating, which is why they were regarded as fungi, but slime moulds are *not* fungi. When we look more closely, we discover a set of independent cells like amoebas. These move around the soil, engulfing bacteria and the like, but then something strange happens.

The cells begin to release a chemical signal which says (basically) 'let's have a party!' When the signal is strong enough, all the cells in an area, often more than 100,000 of them, get together to make something the size of a large slug. At times, it can resemble dog vomit as it creeps over the lawn at about one millimetre an hour, recycling dead stuff. Then when the time is ripe, the white, grey, tan, red, pink or yellow 'mildew' mass makes large numbers of spores and the process starts again.

Sometimes, this mildew-like covering can block the sun from a few grass leaves, so those leaves go yellow which might signal a different disorder, but no real harm is done. A former mycology teacher described to me how somebody I knew (names have been suppressed to protect the guilty), who had been working as a government agriculture and gardening advisor, was less than effective in controlling the problem. When people called this Mr X and described this problem, he always told them to hose it off. This, said my teacher with a grin, made conditions even more suitable for the slime moulds. Even down-trodden slime moulds have their friends— and you, as a lawn lover, can afford to be among them!

FERTILISERS

Some wild ideas on improving the soil to improve plant growth have been offered over the years. One, from one of my favourite nineteenth century oddballs, the 10th Earl of Dundonald, Admiral Thomas Cochrane, was the proposal that Trinidad bitumen might make good manure. This was never tried, though nobody would even consider tarring a lawn today. All the same, there could be worse treatments.

Tradition has it that after the Third Punic War, where Rome was victorious, somewhere around 146 BC, the Romans tore down the Phoenician city of Carthage, ploughed over the ground where the city had stood, and sowed the city's fields with salt to stop anything growing there ever again. It is quite likely that there is a degree of hyperbole about this tale, but the message is clear: when you really hate somebody, put salt in their fields and they will get the message.

So what are we to make of this reversal of conventional wisdom which appeared in *Scientific American* in May 1859?

> **" SALT.—The application of two to four hundred pounds of salt to the acre has been found to be of great advantage in promoting the growth of all plants and trees. Warm soils of the inland districts, and especially those that have been dressed liberally with animal manure, are the most benefited. A dressing of salt upon a grass lawn will often increase growth and thicken-up the plants far more than a coating of animal manure. "**

Sea salt is not just sodium chloride: it is a mixture of salts, though people extracting salt from sea water are skilled in getting out the fraction that is closest to pure sodium chloride. There is, however, no fraction that would be *good* for plants, but the level recommended in the article would probably not be too harmful. At the high end, there would be a pound (454 grams) on a 10 foot (3 metre) square, while at the low end, the square would be 15 feet

(5 metres). While that is more than a pinch of salt, it would probably not kill the grass. The advice, perhaps, is best taken with several grains of salt.

The main needs of a lawn are for nitrogen, phosphorus and potassium, known confusingly as NPK, because chemists use K as the symbol for potassium. Most lawn books quickly skip over this curiosity, saying simply that 'kalium is the Latin for potassium', but the real story of the name is a bit more romantic.

Way back in the early nineteenth century, when only a few elements were known, the initial P had already been used for phosphorus. So when Humphry Davy used a clever method to extract potassium from a crude form of potassium carbonate called 'pot ash', he ran into a naming problem, because P was already taken, and two-letter symbols had not yet been 'invented'.

Back then, everybody loved to make Latin names for things, so pot ash, the result of heating plant material in a pot, was made into a sort of Latin as 'potassium'. Davy thought for a bit and then recalled that pot ash was known in the Arabic science of alchemy as *al kali*. Potash was, in fact, the first alkali, something they used in making soap (an Islamic invention). Anyhow, Davy Latinised that as 'kalium', and K became the symbol for potassium.

Nitrogen is the most available of the three essential nutrients, because it makes up around 80% of the atmosphere, but for most of the living world, atmospheric nitrogen is a total disaster—the gas comes in neat packets of two atoms, which cling tightly to each other. A few microorganisms can split the nitrogen molecules and form 'fixed nitrogen'. These are molecules that combine nitrogen with other elements, and this is the form of nitrogen that plants and animals need.

Some plants, like clovers, have evolved a convenient relationship with their roots forming nodules where these microbes can live, 'fixing' nitrogen and paying the rent by contributing some of it to the landlord plant. When the clover leaves and stems die and rot, the nitrogen goes into the environment—if there is one. If the environment has been degraded enough, it will be time to get out the fertiliser bags, the spreader and all of the other paraphernalia of chemical lawn care.

Once all the fertiliser used on a lawn came from animals, mainly horses, though not entirely. I can still remember the howls of outrage from the neighbours when my father treated his lawn with 'blood and bone'. In the nineteenth and twentieth centuries, guano and Chile saltpetre were transported to Europe and America in large amounts. At first, these were used on fields alone, but later, they came to be used on lawns as well.

Plants have other needs as well, mainly calcium, iron and zinc. They also need a number of other elements in trace amounts, which is why they are called 'trace elements'. Because organic fertilisers come from living things, they generally have enough of the trace elements in them, but this is never certain. That aside, compost often contains weed seeds, so we tend to rely on synthetic fertilisers which are usually derived from large amounts of oil or energy, which amounts to the same thing, given that most of our energy is derived from fossil fuels.

There are more amusing ways to use fertiliser, if you have the right mind set. According to somebody who shall be identified only as 'Connie' (not her real name), some time between 1952 and 1956, her husband was involved in a spraying plot. In those days, as now, there was a degree of rivalry between the University of Texas and Texas A&M (aka the 'Aggies'), and that year, tu (as the Aggies know it) made the mistake of hiring Aggies as summer labour. Regrettably, not all Aggies are as devoid of wit as the tu people thought, and when the Aggie workers were given the task of fertilising the football field, they saw a chance for mischief. A&M had beaten tu rather handily the year before, so the score was written on the grass in fertiliser. The message stood out 'nice and green for some time thereafter'.

THE RISE OF THE MOWER

✤ ✤ ✤

Everybody has their own way of dividing humanity.
Computer geeks say there are 10 types of people: those
who understand binary arithmetic and those who don't.
Trey Rogers sees three kinds of humans: the lawn snobs
who care passionately about their lawns and pay somebody
to maintain everything, the lawn slobs who treat their
grass with disdain, and the lawn geeks, folks with calluses
on their hands and a permanent black line under their nails
as evidence of their commitment to the god, Lawn.

8

Rogers is a turf scientist who, as he describes it, turns out the next generation of lawn geeks. He likens lawn care to dental hygiene, where fertilising and irrigation are the equivalent of brushing and flossing. In his view, you need a mower, fuel cans, a string trimmer (also known as a weed whacker or whipper-snipper, two trade names which now seem to be applied as generics), a spreader, a sprayer, shovels, rakes, a hose, pruning shears and safety goggles. Others would add a dust mask, sprinklers, sieves, a roller and some specialist digging tools. It wasn't always that complicated.

While the scythe had the advantage that the user could stand upright, it was a tool that required (and still requires) great skill to use effectively. It consists of the snath, a long wooden handle and a long, extremely sharp blade which is swung across the ground in long, low and even sweeps.

A beginner has trouble keeping the blade parallel to the ground: this does not matter when grain is being harvested, but it is more of a problem if the scythe is to produce a smooth lawn. The bumps when the blade rises, the divots and nicks where it falls, all contribute to an uneven surface. And until a potential lawn has been cleared of all stones, the paper-thin edge of the blade is at risk as well.

Understandably, most people welcomed alternatives to the scythe. Nowadays, most of us know the scythe as that curious instrument carried by the Grim Reaper but there are enthusiasts around the world who keep the art

of scything alive. There is even an international email list for scythe users, though the list traffic is very low. If your neighbours use one, you would be well advised to keep clear, as scythes are not good for ankles or small animals. They also need to be used with some care around shrubs and trees.

The scythe is still used in the Baltic states of Europe, but it has mostly been replaced by the two-stroke scythe substitute known among other things as a string trimmer, where a tough string can be used to beat grass down, tearing blades and stalks. Along the banks of the Rhine River in Germany, sits a collection of distance markers—one every 100 metres—that are numbered and that extend down to the river's mouth. The grass around them is cleared in a pattern that gave me hope that it may have been scythes used to do the trimming. But when I eventually managed to spot a clearer-of-the-grass in action, he was wielding a string trimmer.

It is always possible that other methods of grass trimming may one day emerge, though some may prove to be too extreme for home use. In 1883, a group of Fenians, bent on seeking Irish independence, entered into what the papers called the 'Dynamite Conspiracy', but the police broke the ring and seized some 200 pounds (about 90 kg) of nitroglycerine. On 12 April of that year, it was decided that the material might be unstable, so it was spread on the ground in a meadow near the Woolwich arsenal in two trickles, one 200 feet long, the other 120 feet long, (call it 60 metres and 40 metres) crossing each other. Most of the material burned safely, but a few stubborn patches remained unignited.

Sure that the earlier fires proved that the material was safe, chemists then went to light the remaining material. But instead of burning, a portion 'exploded, tearing up the earth to a depth of about 18 in. [45 cm], and forming a trench 2 ft. [60 cm] wide, besides raising the turf perceptibly on both sides, and cutting off the grass for some distance as neatly as it might have been done with a lawn-mower'.

This observation does not appear to have led to any new advances in mowing technology. As we have seen earlier, non-exploding sheep mowed many of London's parks in the nineteenth century. In an era when the streets were normally covered in horse dung, a few dried sheep droppings on the grass would have disturbed nobody, and the animal mowers came and went, especially in wartime.

LAWNS IN WAR AND PEACE

In May 1941, *The Times* reported the sound of the first turtle dove and greeted it as a sign of summer, one of 'that category of restful noises which includes the sound of a lawn-mower, the click of croquet balls, and the distant—very distant—whirr of a threshing machine'. The lawn mower referred to was clearly not one that relied on a petrol engine.

In September 1942, *The Times* reported that sheep were grazing the lawns of Versailles. It was, said the paper, to be presumed that the problem was a want of lawn mowers, both human and mechanical.

In late May 1944, the date of the landings in Normandy that would destroy the Nazis was a secret. Still, just a week before D-Day, everybody was sure that the landings would soon begin. Peace in Europe was almost a year off, but the tide had turned. Weary Britons could begin to hope in the middle of 1944 and even begin to care about when there might be lawn tennis again, if they took *The Times*.

Alert to its readers' needs, the paper addressed their concerns. Those with an aged pony might be able to haul a mowing machine over the tennis court, or a person skilled with a scythe might use that, but such people were rare. *The Times* commended rabbits in movable runs, clearing the grass and providing meat for the pot. Others used geese, tethered goats, or hens, and four rams would keep a court nice and short. The best solution, said the paper, was rabbits followed by sheep, to 'keep the turf in good trim for the day when the tennis net goes up again'.

Rabbits were common, as another American friend assured me, recalling her earlier days on the south coast of Oregon. 'When I was a kidlet, Dad raised rabbits. He built a big square pen (I guess the side-boards were 1 x 12) with a chicken wire top and put it out in the yard, then slipped several bunnies inside. When they had fairly well cropped the grass in that area, all he had to do was slide the pen to another place in the yard'.

The suburban lawn did not immediately follow Budding's invention. The new technology had to catch on and shape horticultural fashion. At first, the lawn was a sort of counterpoint to the garden beds and shrubberies, with a neat lawn, somewhere in the middle. What was important was that the mower made a lawn possible for those who lacked the income to maintain a full-time gardener. Then, over time, the lawn mower progressed from something that was pushed with great gusto and effort to something that was pushed gently as a motor did the hard work. Then it became a device that was followed or ridden as it took itself though the grass.

The lawn mower was more subtle as a technology than the railway, the telegraph or the internet, and rather than shaping society, it shaped the environment that society inhabited, so its effects were a little slower in coming. But if the scythe could hang on in some places, by the late 1850s, the lawn mower had been let loose on the world. All that was required was for the public to accept that lawns needed to be mowed, short and often.

At first, most people in the world's more developed countries felt no need of a lawn mower. Their lawns were tiny patches of grass in practical gardens where they grew vegetables for the table, flowers for the house and a few herbs for the pot. A patch of grass like that could be cropped by moving a rabbit hutch around, or it could be scythed, sickled or trimmed with shears, and the product fed to some household animal or other.

When Budding waxed poetic about his mower in 1830, he said it was far better than an old-fashioned scythe: '... the eyes will never be offended by those circular scars, inequalities and bare places, so commonly made by the best mowers with the scythes, and which continue visible for several days'. Soon, the clatter of non-scarring Budding mowers began to be heard in the land.

The problem though, was the clatter. The blades were driven by crude and ill-fitting gears made of cast-iron—this was an age before the invention of machine-cut gears. Still, by 1858, John Ferrabee's son James declared that 7000 Buddings had been sold. It would have been more, he said, were it not for the imitators.

Budding's patent expired in 1855, and the key period for cylinder mowers in Britain lay between about 1856 and 1863. In May 1856, Alexander Shanks of Arbroath in Scotland obtained a patent for a pulled machine, and a month later, Thomas Green of Leeds obtained a patent for a similar mower. There had been pulled machines since 1841, but now they were far more effective—and more important, leather boots had been developed, allowing donkeys and horses to be shod with them so they could tread the lawn, improving it without ripping holes in it.

In 1859, Green added the chain drive that made his Budding-style *Silens Messor* (the Silent Reaper), run more quietly, and in 1863, another firm experimented with a friction drive, using wheels covered in India rubber, but these slipped on wet grass. By 1862, Green already had eight different models out. Now the machines were in place, ready to change society, once society accepted the mower.

In August 1859, *The Times* reported that the Society of Arts Exhibition was impressed by Boyd's patent lawn mower, as exhibited by Mr Samuelson of Banbury. This admirable device was fitted with a bristle brush that cleaned and sharpened the blades as they turned, allowing the mower to be used in wet or dry weather, with no fear of clogging. It could be set to a variety of heights, and was claimed to be able to do the work of half a dozen men, working all day, 'in an hour or two'.

The common date quoted for the first US patents for lawn mowers is 1868, but this is clearly wrong. The confusion has arisen because the word 'reel' has been left out of such claims. The first reel lawn mower patent in the US was indeed issued in 1868, but the pages of *Scientific American* reveal a number of lawn mowers appearing as early as 1863. As with assigning a date to the first lawn mower, the reader needs to be wary not to mistake the agricultural mowers that were being developed during that period for lawn mowers.

In November 1855, a special Prize for Mowing Machines was announced in *Scientific American*. The sum of US$1000 was to be paid to the maker or exhibitor of the best mowing machine. The Trustees of the Massachusetts Society for promoting Agriculture gave inventors a year to prepare for the trial, 'so that the metal and genius of our mowing-machine inventors and makers are thus challenged'. This prize was almost certainly for an agricultural mower.

The same applies to an 1856 report from the same journal. The account almost certainly relates to agricultural machinery, but it shows that the technology, or related technology, was already available in the USA. At a time when lawns were still only occasionally scythed, one of these devices might well have been used on a lawn. That said, the last paragraph seems to make the intended purpose clear, given that farmers bought all of the machines:

" This trial attracted a great number of farmers from different sections of the country, all of whom manifested great interest in the results, and appeared to be satisfied with the benefits of mowing machines, as every machine on the ground was sold on the spot by the agents of them. "

Still, the Age of the American Lawn Mower was close at hand. Henry Fisher's 'hand lawn mower' was offered for sale in September 1863 in *Scientific American*.

" PARTIES DESIROUS OF MANUFACTURING A NEAT One horse Iron Mower, for the Eastern States, or the neatest and lightest Hand Lawn Mower in the world, will please address H FISHER, Canton, Ohio. "

Fisher had considered the task of mowing long grass, and saw that mowers like Budding's reel design required short dry grass. If the grass had been let go until it escaped from the lawn category and leapt into the meadow category, it would be either damp or wet, and the traction wheels would slip. When that happened, regardless of whether the drive was by chain or gears, the blades on the cylinder would fail to turn, and so no mowing would happen.

So Fisher cleverly came up with a set of reciprocating knives, not unlike the action of a modern hedge-trimmer. In this a set of knives was driven by a crank to make one cutting edge glide back and forth past another. He patented his design in May 1863, but by the end of the year, after numerous advertisements in *Scientific American*, offering rights, but to no great effect. Having failed thereafter to either persuade or pay the editors to carry a news story, praising his invention, Fisher placed another advertisement in 1865:

> **" PATENT FOR SALE.—FISHER'S LAWN OR YARD Mower, Patented 1863. Vibrating cutters; lightest machine made, weighs 15 lbs.; a lady can mow with it. For further particulars, address HENRY FISHER, Alliance, Ohio. "**

Here is a patent summary for another early mower, as published in *Scientific American* in August 1865: notice the name given to the machine, and the reference to a 'vibrating cutter'. Once again, it is well before 1868, and once again, it is not a reel or cylinder mower.

> **" 48,947.—Lawn Mowing Machine.—James A. and Henry A. House, Bridgeport, Conn.: We claim the combination of the finger beam frame, vibrating cutter, cam gear and breast piece, arranged and operating substantially in the manner described for the purpose set forth. "**

Finally, we reach patent 73,807, dated January 28 1868, issued to A.M. Hill (strictly, Amariah Millar Hills), which refers to spiral cutters, and now we see the first American reel mower. Here is another description, from February 1868, of the same machine:

> **" LAWN MOWER.—Amariah M. Hill, Hartford, Ct.—This invention relates to a new and improved device for mowing grass by hand, and is more especially designed for mowing lawns. The invention consists in a**

novel manner of constructing the frame of the machine, and inserting it on a roller, whereby the latter is made to have sufficient traction to drive in the most efficient manner the cutting device. The invention also consists in a novel manner of applying the handle to the frame of the machine, whereby the latter may be pushed along by the operator without at all affecting the equilibrium of the machine on its roller; in a novel and improved cutting device, which may be constructed at a very small cost and still be very strong and durable, and not liable to spring during the operation of cutting; and in a peculiar application of these to the device, whereby the height of the cut may be regulated as desired. **99**

We tend to think of our own time as appallingly litigious, but the determined, lemming-like rush of inventors and merchants to enrich lawyers seems to have been no less common in the middle of the nineteenth century, and inventors needed to pay attention to legal precedents. Take this 1865 case as an example: it shows how American inventors were able to take note of British law cases, the account coming from *Scientific American*: the defendant is the maker of the *Silens Messor*.

66 The Lord Chancellor of England has recently decided an important case in the Court of Chancery, involving the rights of joint patentees on appeal from the decision of the Master of the Rolls.

It appeared from the case that the defendant, Thomas Green, had carried on business at Leeds as a manufacturing engineer, and was a maker in particular, of lawn-mowing machines and rollers; and also had a retail shop in Victoria street, Holborn, which was managed by his son, Willoughby Green.
In the latter part of the year 1861, Willoughby Green joined his father at Leeds as partner, when the

London business was carried on by the plaintiff down to the year 1863. Letters-Patent had been obtained in the joint names of the defendants and the plaintiff for improvements in the construction of lawn-mowing machines, etc., and the defendants had been in the habit of granting licenses and receiving royalties on the sale of the machines. In 1863, differences arose between the parties, when the plaintiff filed his bill for an account, claiming, as partner, a share in the royalties received by the defendants, and insisting upon his right to the profits of the London business, which, he alleged, was his own, although carried on in the name of the defendants. 🗩

The plaintiff, who was not named in the *Scientific American* report quoted above, lost his case. Clearly there was money to be made from lawn mowers, enough to make it worthwhile engaging lawyers and pursuing suits and appeals.

MOWERS SPREAD BEYOND BRITAIN

There can be no doubt that by the 1870s, the lawn mower had truly arrived. The demand was there and so was the supply. On 14 May 1870, the *Chicago Tribune* reported a trial of five mowers at Union Park: Hill's, the Excelsior, the Philadelphia, Field's and the Landscape. The judges, appointed by the various manufacturers, agreed unanimously that the Landscape was the best machine, because it was simple and easily worked. The judges also praised the quality of the work.

It is worth diverting here to look at the ways mowers were advertised in the period up to 1875. In January 1873, the Archimedean mower was listed by A.J. Hockings in the Brisbane *Courier* for sale in Australia, along with turf cutters, lawn shears and edging shears. Later in the year, he also offered a British model, 'Green's patent mower' for sale. Here is an account of the Archimedean from *Manufacturer and Builder* in May 1873. Note the references to croquet grounds and the ages for whom the croquet mower is suitable:

" It is durable, simple in construction, and very easily operated. It is perfectly adapted to slopes, undulating lawns, ridges, and valleys, while for croquet-grounds it is invaluable. For the latter purpose, as well as for cemetery lots and similar small inclosures, a special size, known as the croquet-mower, is made, which can be readily worked by a lad or miss of ten years. Every machine is sent from the manufactory properly adjusted, packed, and ready for immediate use. The cutters are so arranged that when dull, they may be quickly and easily sharpened; and when injured, may be replaced by new ones at a small cost. Five sizes of the machine are made, ranging from those of 10-inch cut—suitable for hand-draft—to those of 32-inch cut—designed for horse-power. The prices vary from $20 to $125. The manufacturers are in receipt of a large number of highly laudatory testimonials from both American and foreign journals; though perhaps the best guarantee of the efficiency of the implement is in the fact that while up to the present time over 13,000 have been sold, not one has been returned as unsatisfactory. For further particulars address the Hill's Archimedean Lawn-Mower Company, Colt's Armory, Hartford, Ct. "

The Novelty Lawn Mower offered in 1874 by Geo Dwight of Springfield Massachusetts was hailed as easy to use and 'a reflection on Yankee Ingenuity'. The mower weighed just 20 pounds (9 kg), and cut a 20-inch (50 cm) swathe through the grass, progressing more easily than a 12-inch (30 cm) machine of any other manufacturer, while it could trim close to any corner, vase, tree or door-step, and it cost one-third less. The 'novelty mower' contained a set of reciprocating shears, operated by a crank handle, and resembled the marriage of an egg-beater with a hedge-trimmer, so there was very little about it that was novel.

PEOPLE in the worlds of architecture and landscaping loved the idea of lawn. One writer even suggested that ponies, donkeys or steam engines would soon drive mowers. In fact, it was some 50 years before the first steam mowers began to appear. Animals were already on the job with various pulled machines, but most people had machines that needed a human to push them, and there were many to choose from.

66 Grass-mowing, when long protracted, is one of the most fatiguing occupations, especially when circumstances do not allow the use of the long scythes employed for hay-making, as is often the case on lawns and small grass plots. It is not surprising that Yankee ingenuity invented the small hand-mowing machines, built on the same principle as the large mowers driven by horse-power, and which, by means of a handle, have only to be pulled over the plots in order to cut the grass by means of properly arranged cutters ... All other lawn mowers are heavy, doing damage to grass roots, making it difficult to run them, even for a stalwart man. They require the ground to be prepared for their successful operation, and can only cut short grass; the work of the sickle and shears is about as great with them as without, and they are costly; their scope is limited to the work of a scythe; while this mower can be used under all possible conditions as door-yard trimming. Its price varies from $15 to $20, and is manufactured by Geo. Dwight, Jr. & Co., Springfield, Mass. **99**

Like Henry Fisher's design, Dwight's machines could handle the long grass that a reel mower could not, they were lighter, but in spite of the similarities, the magazine hailed the Novelty as 'an entire departure from the accepted ideas of such implements'. The reciprocating knife mowers were a bit of a side issue, and most manufacturers stayed with cylinders.

While there might be some argument about whether the last two excerpts are advertising or not, this piece from *Manufacturer and Builder* in 1875 has a distinctly advertorial feel to it. It quacks like a duck, it walks like a duck, and even from upwind, it has the distinctive aroma of a duck.

66 The lawn mower, in its various forms, has been before the public for so many years that it is here unnecessary to dwell upon the great saving of time and labor which it causes over the slow and laborious work of the hand-sickle or scythe; indeed it is impossible to produce with the latter implements, unless they are handled with no small degree of skill, the smooth and velvety lawns so easily and quickly gained by the aid of the mower. As is the case with all such useful inventions, there are many varieties in the market, each of which presents some especial merits in its construction. Out of the number however with which we are familiar, we know of none more worthy of the notice of our readers than that which forms the subject of our accompanying illustration.

Any one who has seen the perfect condition in which grass-plots and lawns are kept where the grass is cut with a mechanical mower, attached to a roller, moved over the ground, will be convinced of the desirableness of such a contrivance, of which our fathers knew nothing, and thus had to submit to the labor of cutting the grass with a sickle, a very hard task when a large surface has to be gone over, while a mechanical mower may be rolled over the ground, requiring no more effort than is consistent with a healthy exercise, while for a strong, active person it is equivalent to a mere toy.

The advantages of this mower are claimed to be that it runs lightly, rolls the ground, cuts the borders, needs little repair, cuts very high grass, its adjustments are simple, the gears are perfectly covered, while the roller does not run in the standing grass. A great aid and advantage is that every one of the twenty-five parts of which the mower is made up, can be replaced at an expense of from 30 cents to $3. These parts are all separately marked with letters, and all that one has to do is to report to the manufacturer what part has been damaged or destroyed, whether it be a roller, a knife, a handle, a bolt, or other part, to have the same sent, when it will at once fit into its place, as all the parts are made

alike for the different sizes of the machine; the charge is made according to a fixed and very reasonable price-list, sent with the instructions or directions for using and preserving it. These mowers are made by the Chadborn & Coldwell Manufacturing Co., of Newburgh, N. Y. 99

By 1875, the need for mower service led to a new nuisance that might have resulted, sooner or later in a court case. One J. Goulton-Constable of Walcott-Hall, Brigg, Lincolnshire, wrote to *The Times* to complain that he had five times sent his lawn mower back to Messrs Shanks in London to have it repaired. Each time it had been returned as rail freight, each time arriving broken.

66 **Comment appears to me to be needless. I only hope, Sir, that you will publish this in order that those through whose negligence these five successive breakages have occurred may see it and feel ashamed of themselves.** 99

Reginald Beale noted in 1931 that Messrs Ransomes of Ipswich were the first to manufacture lawn mowers on a commercial scale '... and tradition says that their first machine was tried on my lawn at Teddington some sixty years ago'—that is, around 1870. In fact, the Ransomes company made its first Budding-style models under licence in 1832 when Ferrabee was unable to keep up with demand.

By 1882, the mown lawn was a given in civilised society. *Harper's Monthly* could describe the mountains of San Juan (south-western Colorado) as being 'as rounded and smooth on top as if they had been shaved with a lawn mower', confident that readers would understand the meaning. Then in January 1886, *American Missionary* reported the donation of one Buckeye junior lawn mower, made in Springfield Ohio, to Talladega College in Alabama.

Talladega was a college for the people we now call African Americans, but while an educator might think books would be more to the point, the good folk of Ohio must have wanted to see Talladega become as civilised as 'The Lawn', the name by which the University of Virginia was universally known. Perhaps lawn mowers must also have had an improving side. Mary Caroline Robbins certainly thought tidy lawns were a good start in civilising the Great Unwashed. She hailed a variety of improvements in *The Atlantic Monthly* in 1896:

> “ A simple but lively agent in the movement we chronicle has been the general introduction of the lawn-mower, which has made a rough dooryard as old-fashioned in many a village as the unsightly fences of former days, while the supply of water by aqueducts helps to preserve a uniform greenness in the little smooth lawns graded to the edge of the highway. Thus we see how one advance leads imperceptibly to another, till the whole great scheme is evolved. ”

In the same year, an American poet named Hayden Carruth revealed in a fictional work in *Harper's New Monthly Magazine* just how common the lawn mower was. Even poets knew about them by 1882, and the merest menial was expected to be able to operate one. Here is the start of Carruth's story'

> **“ But, Doctor,' I protested, 'what is the man good for? You say he can't milk, can't drive, doesn't know how to take care of carriages or horses, broke the lawn-mower the first time he tried to use it, and is unable to distinguish between a cabbage-plant and a California redwood. What is his strong point? ”**

We know what the weak point of the mower was: lawn needed constant mowing, because if it got away, pushing a mower through it was hard work indeed. Then it needed the strength of a draught animal—or a machine. From there, it would be a long and downhill track to leaf blowers, lawn vacuum cleaners and all sorts of other clever ways of creating labour so that devices could be used to save it.

✠ ✠ ✠

POWERED MOWERS

✻ ✻ ✻

At first, large tracts of grass, parks and playing fields,
were cut by horse-drawn mowers, more closely related to
agricultural implements than to cylinder mowers.
The suburban lawn was mowed with a machine that was
a lineal descendant of the original Budding mowers, and
pushed by a human, but they were on the way out.

In February 1919, *The Times* reported the death of 'Mortlake', a horse which had for 20 years worked at the model farm attached to the cheerily named 'Royal Home and Hospital for Incurables' at Putney. The horse had been foaled there, and was a great friend to all the inmates (as patients were then called). His only fault, said the report, was not liking the leather shoes he had to wear while hauling the large lawn mower. The hospital was hoping that some kind person might provide a replacement.

That hope was unlikely to be satisfied, because by 1919, engines were beginning to replace horses. In the world's armies, cavalry squadrons were becoming tank or air force squadrons; on the world's streets and roads, coaches, carriages and buggies were being replaced by motor vehicles of one sort or another; on the golf courses and parks of the world, tractors towed the mowing machines, not horses.

Horse-drawn mowers were made until 1939, and I saw a buffalo-pulled mower, just a few years ago. Those oddities aside, by 1920, the horse was about to be relegated to a lesser role. It was to be a hobby object, used for expensive recreational riding or even more expensive recreational racing. Like lawns, the horse was no longer a utility, but had become something to pour money into.

The idea of a motorised mower emerged in the early twentieth century. In 1892, James Sumner produced the first steam-powered lawn mower, and after modifications in 1895, it weighed 1.5 tons. In 1902, Alexander Shanks produced the world's first ride-on steam mower, but it had certain

drawbacks. The worst of these was that it put the operator's head about 10 feet (3 metres) above the ground.

This was soon amended to a ride-behind mower design, where something like a steam tractor took the place of the horse. There were certainly petrol-driven mowers in 1896, and the first commercial petrol-powered mower was released in Britain by Ransomes in 1902. With a cut of 42 inches (1070 mm), and with a 6 hp (4.5 kW) engine, this was no toy for young damsels. This was a brutal, thundering macho machine, and the short-lived steam mower died out soon after.

But consider the popular image of Boadicea, the British warrior queen who supposedly rode her chariot at the Romans with scythe-like blades fitted to her wheels. I have often thought that her chariot might really have been the first ride-on mower, even if she sought to mow Romans, rather than grass.

Sadly, the legend of Boadicea's chariot is a recent invention and no surviving remnants of British chariots show any sign of blades being fitted. This is a pity, as I had formed an interesting hypothesis about the way short garden gnomes evolved in Britain, in the same way that short rosette weeds were selected by the mowing machines of the twentieth century.

At the Royal Botanic Society in London's Regent's Park in 1904, a certificate of merit went to Ransomes, Sims and Jefferies of Ipswich for their lawn mowers. The firm also gave an exhibition during the afternoon on the lawns on either side of the broad walk. Here, they ran their motor-driven mowers to considerable acclaim.

The bigger machines might also serve as lawn rollers, given their huge weight, but now the roller, once moved by a man, or at a pinch by a pony in leather boots, could swell in size. On large properties and cricket pitches, rollers were propelled by larger engines, filled with water ballast, and some even came fixed with spikes to aerate the soil, but as the suburban lawn spread its influence, rollers were usually hauled by hand. Many mowers, on the other hand, were still too large to be propelled by a human.

In July 1916, in the midst of war, *The Times* noted that with a general shortage of skilled men to do gardening, lawn owners would need to shift for themselves. Lawns would be going to seed, said the writer, and needed mowing, but in the era when mechanised war was only just emerging, the horses had all gone off to war as well. Those people '... who possess a small light car geared to go at five miles an hour or less' were advised to use it to tow a mowing machine over the lawn.

'Half an hour's practice should be enough to establish a working understanding between the man or woman at the wheel and the individual guiding the mower. The inevitable wheel marks will soon disappear'. It seems that in an era before mechanised war, fuel for vehicles was easily available.

Sadly, the lack of gender-specific language represented neither a dip of the hat in Boadicea's direction nor even a small degree of enlightenment at *The Times*. We will see how *The Times* saw a woman's role in the next chapter, when we look at the Astors' picnic for the newspaper's staff. No, the language was just a nod to the unusual times brought on by a war that had removed so many able-bodied males. Normality would be restored and women moved back off the lawns, just as soon as peace returned.

NEW WAYS OF MOWING

Fuel was in very short supply in World War II. In June 1943, *The Times* reported that with the shortage of petrol for mowing machines, many lawns had turned into miniature hayfields. After the war ended, the old hand-managed machines were mostly thought to be too heavy and cumbersome.

What was needed was a new way of mowing, and so we come to two petrol-powered inventions which, though they were easier to use, were far more able to injure their users: the rotary mower and the ride-on mower.

These days, most of us have left behind the whirling cylinder of the precision reel mower with a trailing roller. This would travel across the grass, picking up each leaf and cutting it with its rotary shears. We have replaced its neat snipping with the thuggish and brutal rotary action of a flywheel with two lumps of metal, blunt blades that batter and bruise the grass, ripping leaves away.

The rotary mower was an obvious idea, but it was held back until the development of a light engine capable of moving the tip of the blade fast enough—170 mph (270 kph) was the blade speed needed to cut grass. Any slower, and the grass would bruise and bend, but it would not be cut through.

True, a scythe moves more slowly, but the action of the blade sees it sliding sideways as it pushes through the grass. That one little speed fact also puts paid to my notion of Boadicea's chariot mowing the grass by pushing scythes through it. By 1930, motors were efficient enough to deliver the requisite speed, and the first rotary mowers began appearing in Britain. Soon, stones were flying, and feet were being run over.

The rotary machines had several drawbacks. There is no roller trailing behind, conveniently located between the operator and the operation and able to intercept flying objects. More importantly, the lack of a roller meant there was no way to smooth the grass out. That rules out any chance to make neat patterns to satisfy the operator's artistic whimsy. To this day, when you look at a playing field and see neat stripes in the grass, this is a result of the roller behind the mowing machine, operated by an intelligent driver.

Sadly, if some people have their way, there may soon be no human input at all, as robot mowers take over, prowling randomly across the garden, searching out long grass and massacring any blade of grass that dares raise its head above the established standard height.

Husqvarna released two styles of robot mower in 1993, one (the more expensive) being deemed more 'ecological' because it uses solar power (we will carefully avoid questions about the carbon cost of the mower and the cells). The proud owners of some of these need to mark out a perimeter with wire, and plants and flower beds can be designated as no-go areas in the same way. Since then, other models have been released, but most of these also require a perimeter wire.

With the falling price of consumer electronics, it would probably be as easy (and cheaper) to have the mower fitted with GPS, accessing a precision map of areas where the machine is permitted or not. The map could be downloaded from the home computer, and transferred either by Bluetooth or by a USB thumbstick.

Remember that you read it here first, but while that sort of complicated system may appeal to early adopters, geeks and ageing info-hippies like me, I have to suspect it will never catch on with the traditional mob. The robots can not cut short enough and neatly enough to satisfy the purists.

There is another drawback to the use of a computer or robot: part of the lawn-mowing experience is to let the urban male pretend to be an agricultural breadwinner. Like the fake pastoralism of Marie Antoinette, parading her sheep, the mower-rider can dream of being productive as he rides his faux-tractor around the grass, maybe even singing cowboy songs to it.

Like sheep, say the robot makers, the robots might be vulnerable to thieves, so like sheep, the robots will emit an electronic bleat if they are carried off. What those makers probably do not know is that early Australian explorers knew about bleating. They preferred to take goats into the wilderness as food animals when travelling as they had observed that goats do in fact bleat when they are carried off, unlike sheep. It seems that even the robot makers have left their agrarian roots too far behind.

The users of mowers have also left behind their hunter-gatherer roots, acquired in a time when humans had to assume that everything in their environment was out to get them. How else can we explain some of the things that people allow their mowers to do to them?

MOWER ACCIDENTS

One thing is certain: with the arrival of rotary and ride-on mowers, the number of mowing accidents each year rose alarmingly. To be fair, though, even before lawn mowers became common, there were deaths caused by mowers of the human sort, and no doubt there have been a few cases of people being attacked by frisky animals whose primary role was as mowers.

In June 1858, Charles Hodder was employed to mow clover with scythes in a field near Sherborne in England. The human mowers all stopped for refreshment and to sharpen their scythes. When they were done, Hodder lay down and fell asleep. 'The mower who worked next to the deceased did not perceive his companion lying against the swathe of grass which he was cutting, and the first stroke of his sithe (sic), carrying its burden to the swathe, drove its point deep into the neck of the poor fellow ...' Hodder's jugular vein was severed, and he bled to death. He left behind a widow and five orphaned children.

Even when there was no power to the mower, death could come unexpectedly. In June 1920, Albert Worrell was working as a gardener at Stoneleigh Abbey in Warwickshire. A storm arose and he sheltered in a hollow under a tree, sitting on his lawn mower, where he was struck dead by lightning.

THE LAWN MOWER AS MINCER

Towards the end of World War I, Britons were tired of the war. They were tired of untidy grass as well, and one eccentric combined the two into a general solution that recalled the risks mower operators take. There were, in fact, many eccentric ideas that were reported with a straight face in the *Ministry of Munitions Journal*.

Foremost were schemes to artificially freeze clouds so guns might be mounted on them, though other inventors wanted to suspend them from large balloons, in either case, gaining a height and range advantage. Balloons were also to be used to obscure the moon, though others thought they could do this better with a 'black beam'.

Inspired by the recently invented tank, somebody proposed disposing of the Germans by letting loose 'a machine of the nature of a lawn mower as large as a Tank to make mincemeat of them'. Clearly, somebody in Britain knew all about the nefarious effects of a rogue mower coming into contact with flesh.

Wartime always brought out the strangest of ideas in people with too much spare time. Neighbours were accused of sending signals to foreign aircraft or submarines by the arrangement of their washing, though nobody seems to have been accused of using their lawn mower to make messages, yet in Arthur Ransome's 1943 book, *Picts and Martyrs*, Nancy used a lawn mower to write a message to Dick and Dorothy. Perhaps people with suspicious minds were above reading children's literature. The lawn that Nancy mowed, by the way, was 'half of it level, where once upon a time people had played lawn tennis or croquet, and half of it sloping down to the river'. Times were changing.

Still if the first blood was drawn by the mowers early on, the carnage was nothing to that wrought by the ride-on mower. It went through a number of harmless forms first, but even these could hurt the unwary. The idea was by no means new: agricultural mowing machines, used on crops, typically had reciprocating knife action, and a seat for the person controlling the horse which pulled the machine. When a Mr Worthington of Shawnee USA took several cylinder mowers in 1919 and ganged them behind a horse to mow parks and playing fields, nothing could be more natural than to add a seat. By 1920, this design was available in Britain.

The early petrol mowers carried themselves forward, eliminating the drudgery of pushing them, while still leaving the operator the trudgery of walking behind them. Soon after World War I, rollers were sold in England with a seat attached. For those with push mowers, there was a brief vogue for motorised mower-pushers, which were linked rigidly to the push mower, and once again, offered a seat to the operator.

In the early 1960s, came a strange English device with a bicycle seat, the Anzani Lawnrider, but that was eclipsed soon after by the release in the USA of the tractor-shaped ride-on mower, and John Deere followed soon after. Today, only serious lawnsmen of a certain age and nationality would recall the Lawnrider.

Many, though, have had the chance to recall the tractor-style mower with some bitterness. It is a cantankerous machine which needs to be suited to the wetness of the grass, and this explains why US models are rare in the British Isles, but more importantly, the 'ride-on' is an inherently unstable machine, as any tractor is, but it is one that will inevitably be ridden by an inexperienced driver. On any sort of slope, older models are likely to overturn and may rend their riders with whirling blades. To give the makers their due, more recent builds have safety features like engine cut-outs.

THE DENVER-SERLING CONNECTION

John Denver knew all about mowing injuries. As a young man, he was injured in a motor mower accident, and so was classified 1-Y by the US military. This meant that he never served in the forces, yet he is often said (on fan websites) to have been a sniper in Vietnam. You might say he was saved by the mower, though it was a fairly extreme salvation, as the accident took off two of his toes.

Movie producer Rod Serling, on the other hand, did not have a lawn mower accident as such, but suffered a massive heart attack in 1975 while mowing, and he died soon after. In 2004, a survey of legends of science fiction put him at the top, the only human among 24 fictional characters. Yet for all that he wrote futuristic science fiction, he died attending to an outmoded and unnecessary mowing imperative, a throwback to an agrarian past which serves no useful purpose now, and which will serve no useful purpose in the future.

The statistics (and as we will see, tales) of lawn mower accidents are at best dubious, but the following appears to be a reasonably reliable set of frequently asserted 'facts'. For starters, Canada has around 100 lawn mower accidents each year that result in amputation or serious bleeding. The most believable figures seem to suggest that the US has just under 80,000 mower accidents a year. All the same, the authoritative Standards Australia is willing to quote a report that 'every year in the US there are 100,000 injuries due to power lawn mowers—and that 11 per cent of these happen to children under 15 years of age'.

So now we have a report of a report of a report. There is, as you can see, a problem in verifying the numbers and getting to primary data. What we know for certain is that a rotary mower spins at around 3000 rpm, a force which can generate three times the muzzle velocity of a .357 magnum pistol, a firearm designed to penetrate vehicles and even the people inside them.

If you give that sort of speed to a pebble or some other small item in the grass, the results can be disastrous. In a study of ER admissions in the US, 12,000 cases over eight years were examined, and injuries were found to be mainly from flying debris, followed by people trying to fix mowers while the engine was running. Most hospitalisation cases seemed to involve broken or amputated toes.

EVEN in the 1950s, mowers in advertisements were operated by women with the legs of Barbie-the-doll, and the pneumatic torso of a starlet. From a close examination, it appears that they were all fitted with either hooks or Velcro on their upper arms. These fixture were never visible, but only a firm anchorage at a point below the shoulders could possibly account for the way their off-the-shoulder and unbuttoned blouses did not obey the law of gravity.

The picture is muddied for the dedicated researcher by the hyperbole of ambulance-chasing lawyers who cheerily paint gloomy pictures of the ghastly injuries suffered from operating a ride-on mower when the mower rolls, if the machine lacks an engine cut-out.

The US Consumer Product Safety Commission (CPSC) says that in 2003, there were more than 76,000 cases requiring treatment in hospital emergency rooms, clinics, and doctors' surgeries, and there were 23 cases of over-65s being killed in lawn mower accidents when they fell off the mower, rolled it, or ran it over a drop of some sort.

Some of the alleged injuries lack any substance, like the persistent urban myth about 'the man who used his mower as a hedge trimmer'. The usual version has a foolish man noticing that his hedge needed a trim, and because he had no hedge trimmer, raising his mower to manoeuvre it along the top of the hedge, losing four fingers in the process. The yarn is one of those silly lawsuit/silly law/silly lawyer yarns where the victim then sues the manufacturer (and wins) because there was no warning on the mower that said it should not be used as a hedge trimmer. The finger-loss part sounds somewhat plausible, but the lawsuit part is most improbable.

In those cases where there really was an apparently silly lawsuit, like the famous case of the lady who got a lap full of hot coffee and won against McDonald's, the story only sounds silly because key features are left out of it, features that changed the nature of the case. As a rule, lawyers proceed in a sensible and logical way to a conclusion that is consistent with justice and also with past decisions. There is no way the courts are going to open Pandora's box and establish a regime in which I can sue because the manufacturer of my computer failed to warn me against using my computer as an ear-ring or as a parachute.

The lawn mower hedge-trimmer case is often cited for the Darwin awards (given to those who improve humanity by removing themselves from the human gene pool). It may be cited, but there is absolutely no evidence at all that any such lawsuit was ever brought, and even less evidence that it was ever won! If ever a case had merit, it would have to be that of mower operators employed by Tiger Time Lawn Care in Memphis Tennessee if they are ever injured. Tiger Time employees include young woman in bikinis who can be booked to come and mow one's lawn. Anybody who has seen them, or film of them is likely to worry that their attire falls short of the industrial standards for such work.

It is just possible that the operators do, in fact, wear suitable protective footwear. I have only seen short clips of them working, and the angles used (the camera angles seem to hover on the torso region) are singularly lacking in detail on their feet. While the normal sweaty and skinny males do most of the work for Tiger Time, there is a special service that can be called for.

THE ART OF SELLING

The bikini mowers appear to be in part a publicity gimmick. The ploy has certainly managed to get Tiger Time onto Youtube and assorted 'current affairs' TV shows, where it was marketed as something for women to order as a special 'treat' for a male relative. It seems that the male was expected to sit back, sip on a beer, and hope for a wardrobe malfunction. Even though mowing is a male prerogative, there seems to be a lurking fantasy here, but to one who has spent much of his life trying to prevent accidents in laboratories and the like, I am afraid my masculine urges stand no chance against the concern I feel for unprotected feet.

As advertisers know, sex sells. Almost all of the pictures of mowers shown in technical journals in the nineteenth century show the mower being operated by a slim man or even a boy. The various library collections of trade cards—coloured illustrations handed out to potential buyers— that appear to have been widely used for the promotion of lawn mowers, seem always to show young ladies in costumes which, given the norms at the time of printing, are surprisingly abbreviated in the hemline area. Then again, given that men were the most likely purchasers of lawn mowers, perhaps the glimpses of ankle given by the models were not so surprising after all. Not quite lawn porn, perhaps, but moving in that direction.

I don't wish to suggest here that the women were in any way impractical. Unlike the Tiger Time ladies, you could generally see their footwear, and they always wore high stiletto heels, which obviously would allow them to aerate the lawn as they mowed, rather than having to get out a fork or a spiked roller. That said, rollers of various sorts were always available to the serious lawnsman. Some could have weight added, some were motorised, and some were spiked, so they drilled a series of holes in the soil, about 1 inch (2.5 cm) deep. Forks could also be used to open up the soil, but a roller was essential, and ideally, the tines were hollow, so that they removed a small plug of soil.

I am not sure if Mortlake the horse ever pulled a roller at London's Royal Home and Hospital for Incurables, but it is likely he did. In my younger days, I played hockey, the sport that North Americans call 'field hockey'. Back then, it was played on grass, and like maternal and paternal cousins and my wife's cousins, I knew that the best field in Sydney was in the grounds of a local 'mental asylum' where a number of the patients spent a lot of energy hauling a heavy roller over the turf, except when the field was being used.

Once or twice, patients made moves to use it while a game was in progress, but they were generally dissuaded. I have no idea how the mower was operated. But it was a different time and I almost suspect that hauling a heavy mower might have been seen as appropriate therapy. I do know that up until perhaps 1960, rollers were traditionally considered essential, especially on turf cricket pitches. In fact, they are used to this day for all matches at a higher level.

When Mr Stephenson-Peach invented the first electric mower, in 1896, he faced the same problem that a Renaissance inventor of bicycle pumps would have faced. There was no real market, because so few people had electricity available in their houses, but in the 1950s, battery and mains electric mowers reappeared.

Inspired by this, my father made an electric lawn mower from the motor of a discarded vacuum cleaner, wood, pram wheels and two hacksaw blades. He also made his own roller using several bags of cement and a 4 gallon (20 litre) drum. The handle was made of water pipe, but while I say 'his own roller', that is slightly inaccurate.

I was a slight youth, a sort of stunted willow; the unkind might even have called me puny. My father declared that the electric mower was too skittish for me or anybody else to use—indeed, even he discarded it entirely after a close encounter between the blade and the power cord. On the other hand, he considered the roller just right for his emaciated son who needed only some exercise to develop magnificent pectorals.

He would order loads of 'top dressing', barrow the soil into place and spread it, then leave me to do the hauling of the roller, back and forth. The bumps on the ground would soon disappear, but none appeared in or around my musculature.

Some people appear to have prospered, even thrived, under the roller's burden. When the Reverend George John Hammon died in 1922, England apparently saw the passing of one of its eccentrics. Having served in five curacies, he purchased the advowson of Chacombe, a small village near Banbury. This gave him the right to appoint the vicar, and when the position fell vacant in 1894, he appointed himself, as was his right. He was aged 63.

What followed can be read between the lines: there were, said *The Times*, 'disputes in the village' and Hammon was sometimes the only one at services, discharging the duties of vicar, organist, verger and bellringer until 1914, when he retired at the age of 83, and appointed a successor, but continued for some years wielding a scythe and hauling a 10-hundredweight (half-ton) roller.

We credit Ralph Waldo Emersion with the saying about people beating a path to your door if you build a better mousetrap, but the quotation is somewhat incorrect. In in 1855, he wrote in his journal:

> " I trust a good deal to common fame, as we all must. If a man has good corn, or wood, or boards, or pigs, to sell, or can make better chairs or knives, crucibles, or church organs, than anybody else, you will find a broad, hard-beaten road to his house, though it be in the woods. "

Many of the commodities Emerson listed are no longer in demand, and the same goes for mousetraps. Still, if you need a broad path beaten to your house today, consider inventing a new device for weeding lawns—or doing anything else on lawns—and stand back to avoid the rush.

Of course, when the original Stately Home lawn that we all strive to imitate was established, there would have been no mower as we know it, no hoses and no sprays. Today, these are the key items, and to a certain extent, the other tools and devices are just there for show.

Australians may venerate their Victa mowers as icons, asserting that one of their own, Mervyn Victor Richardson, invented the design. The Victa was a far better design than what went before, but it was not the *first* rotary mower. The Australian reverence for the Victa is nothing to the way Americans love their John Deere brand. They wear John Deere mesh caps and ride John Deere bicycles. They can even have lawn sprinklers shaped like John Deere tractors, while the truly committed have mail boxes in the same shape.

Children can start out on John Deere tractor rockers and progress to ride-on toys with a loader and bucket, powered by a 6-volt motor. These items all say one thing to the casual passer-by: here lives a man who cares about his lawn, a man who is instilling the eternal verities of lawnsmanship into his offspring! In the USA, such products are better than lawn pets of any sort, and Mr Veblen would be pleased at their inordinate costliness.

RIDE 'EM, MOWBOY!

Ride-on mowers have other uses. The British Lawn Mower Racing Association (BLMRA) reports that it was founded in 1973 at the Cricketers Arms in Wisborough Green, West Sussex. Jim Gavin, an Irish race and rally driver, was disgruntled that the cost of racing was in an upward spiral, thanks mainly to sponsorship. This meant the way into motor racing was blocked for ordinary amateur enthusiasts.

And so it came to pass that a group of drinkers, downing their pints, looked across the village green to where the green keeper was mowing the field, using a ride-on mower. Here, they agreed, was a form of vehicle which would lend itself to a cheap and accessible motor sport. After all, they agreed, everybody had a lawn mower in their garden shed.

Unknown to them, similar races had been tried in Pennsylvania in 1955, but this news would not have put them off. They set some standards that hold to this day: no sponsorship, no commercialism, no cash prizes and no modifying of engines; thus keeping costs down. In no time, says the BLMRA, a championship was held in a local farmer's field and up to 80 competitors turned up for a very successful event. They now claim 'up to

250 members', racing in towns and villages across Britain, with twelve dates in their calendar, and even a 12-hour endurance race.

Today, there are four classes from Group 1, push mowers to Group 4, with visible bonnets. Group 2 are tow-behinds, lowered for racing, Group 3 are Lawn Bugs. The safety standards are good, but the sport will probably never be as safe as the drills of the Lawn Rangers of Arcola Illinois. These are broad-brush satirists who need have little fear of ever being taken seriously as they march in a sort of formation, pushing mowers and wielding brooms. Since 1981, they say, more than 1000 men have marched in the LR ranks.

Perhaps it's the name, the decorations on their mowers, the masks or the occasional grass skirt—or their motto: 'You're only young once, but you can always be immature' that gives the game away. Still, the amusement they bring stems from our understanding that the lawn mower in America is profoundly democratic. Like the drinkers at the Cricketers' Arms, everybody has a mower and a lawn. That is probably also why the Sydney Olympics featured Victa mowers.

FUN ON THE LAWN

Kitsch seems to go well with well-kept grass. Lawn decorations seem far more a possession of US lawns, though Paul Meisel hedged his bets when he commented, 'Though lawn ornaments seem to be unique to the United States, little has been written on their history'. I have to agree on both counts.

Only the USA has swarms of pink lawn flamingos. An estimated 20 million of the original version of the pink lawn flamingo were made in the USA during their initial reign. They began slowly as souvenirs of Florida from the 1920s, but when Donald Featherstone made a clay model of a flamingo in 1957, based on a photograph in National Geographic, the real craze began. It ended in 2006 when the maker, Union Products of Leominster, Massachusetts, went out of business. Luckily for kitsch lovers, other manufacturers have since increased their output to maintain supplies. In 2007, the copyright and the moulds were sold, so the pink lawn flamingos will not, it seems, go the way of the dodo just yet.

Elaine Viets clearly understands the nature of lawn mystique. In her 1999 mystery, *The Pink Flamingo Murders*, the first victim was a crabby old man who painted his house purple, the second victim was the local drug dealer, and the third was a socialite who was 'whacked with a pink lawn flamingo'. Clearly, somebody with a sense of neighbourhood improvement has got a little carried away, and the heroine is on the job, seeking out the killer. Some of us might be moved to ask 'Why bother?'

In an interview, Viets explained that it *was* possible to kill with a pink lawn flamingo, and offered a dark warning: 'Did you know that it's not illegal to carry a concealed flamingo in all fifty states, but it is against the law to display them on your lawn in many areas?' To her, visible flamingos are clearly better than those kept out of sight for evil purposes.

Remember Veblen, who recommended that people replace their grazing mowers with something which offered no profit? It turns out that when young Thorstein was only ten years old, the practice of keeping non-profit animals was already common.

A number of European countries had tried to farm the alpaca and the llama for profit. In August 1867, somebody signing himself AJD wrote to *The Times* about the Australian experience with these animals. I have been unable to identify the writer, but he was clearly an Australian in England who had been active among the alpaca growers of Australia. He wanted to advise that experiments with alpacas had been a failure everywhere, especially in Australia, and he suggested that they were best relegated to the role of 'lawn pets'. The term needed no explanation.

Such pets, however, require care and maintenance, so most people took refuge in low-maintenance statuary: cast iron stags, plastic flamingos and concrete geese among them. The concrete geese are an ongoing delight in parts of America, where it is even possible to buy clothing for the birds, a practice which surely has its origins in Alan Abel's antics with the Society for Indecency to Naked Animals.

Read the society's name again. That name alone should have been enough to alert people that the society, outwardly composed of eccentrics and misfits who wanted desperately to clothe nude and lewd animals, was a satire, a leg-pull. All SINA had going for it was a set of poker-faced individuals, a few drawings and the absurd proposition that any animal standing more than 4 inches (10 cm) high or which was more than 6 inches (15 cm) long, should be clothed. For decency's sake!

More recently, Abel has written about his exploits on his website (alanabel.com) and expressed his regret that the American public-at-large was willing to accept SINA as genuine and dismiss them as oddballs, rather than seeing the activity as a biting satire on censorship and repression in the USA. So those who clothe their concrete geese may be the *crème de la crème* of cutting-edge social satire, or they may be blind followers of a sad fashion in grotesque kitsch. Or the population may include a mix of the two. Who can say?

Then again, there may be a hidden meaning. Near my home, there is a supermarket where a single female who places a bunch of bananas pointing upwards in her trolley is supposedly indicating that she is available if there are any interested single males. I suspect that a clever Banana Marketing Board person started the rumour, but it has now passed into Australian folklore, and for all I know, into Australian mating habits.

THE CASE OF JOQUE GRAVES

Bananas and lawns may be unrelated, but there is a resonance with one of the other kitsch items seen in the USA, the 'lawn jockey'. This is a small male figure, dressed in riding silks usually with a black face. Some people claim that this may once have had a hidden meaning. If you dig around, you can find firm assertions that the black-faced statues, apparently racist (or at least non-PC) kitsch have a deeper and much more humanitarian significance. According to a number of web sources, the original was a statue of one Joque Graves, a 12-year-old African-American boy who perished of the cold holding a lantern and guarding some horses, while serving George Washington.

You can read that the grateful general had the statue made later to commemorate the lad's bravery, but there's more: in the run-up to the US Civil War, we are told that the 'lawn jockeys' were used as clandestine signalling devices on the Underground Railroad that took slaves north. Flags, lanterns in certain positions and/or red and green ribbons on the statue told important stories.

OK, I am willing to swallow that, *and* the hypothesis that lawn flamingos stop malaria, that those lawn statues of Mexicans with burros are air navigation devices for UFOs and that the true role of a plaster copy of Michelangelo's 'David' statues on a lawn is classified, but determined by the presence or absence of a fig leaf. It's all on the web, so it must be true!

(After writing that, I enquired further and learned that even if the lawn jockey tale is popular, it is patently false. My informants told me the escapees on the Underground Railroad would be moved at night, when coloured signals would be impossible to see, the red-green stop-go standard that we use now developed long after the Civil War was over, Joque Graves never existed, and the 'jockeys are, in any case, just an outgrowth of the hitching posts required outside each American house in the nineteenth century'.)

One can certainly buy a wide variety of clothing patterns and ready-made clothing for concrete geese, together with appropriately scaled hockey sticks, guns and fishing rods. I have not, to date, been able to find any clothing for tyre swans, a native Australian lawn adornment, now sadly endangered.

Tyre swans are (or were) made from vehicle tyres, but after repeated amputations and eviscerations, Australians have learned that there are things you can do with a fabric-belted tyre that just don't work on modern steel-belted radials. Basically, you have to cut the tyre, then turn it inside out, and neither action is aided by the steel belting. Some say that the tyres of certain motor scooters are good swan material, but the supply is limited.

If lawn is the two-dimensional control of nature, topiary takes the taming of nature to three dimensions. The third dimension gives a great deal more room for whimsy for those so inclined. Some topiarists prefer the sobriety of geometrical shapes, mainly cones and spheres, but there will always be those who seek to sculpt the plants, to provide living green statuary. In 1591, the Earl of Hertford had (as we will see shortly) topiary on his park and in 1599, it was a feature of Hampton Court, where twiggy, leafy green men, women, centaurs and serving maids with baskets were to be seen and admired.

Topiary is seen as quintessentially English, but the idea of a lawn decorated with topiary may well have been conceived first by the French. Where it began matters little because topiary is popular in many other places, and nowhere more whimsically than at Ayutthaya in Thailand, where the royal palace of the King of Thailand features many brilliant examples, especially a small herd of elephants which proceed across the perfect lawn.

Topiary is just hedging gone wrong. The classic hedge is constructed on straight lines, with the occasional smooth curve. Hedges always have flat tops, but now and then, a gardener feels the need to clip a bush into a neat sphere, cone or triangle, and then the game is on for young and old.

The Times did not approve of topiary in 1907: 'The only rule about clipping trees or shrubs is that it should always be done not as unnatural ornament, but for some good practical reason, and when the reason is obvious the clipped tree very seldom looks ugly, and often has a peculiar charm of its own'. William Robinson, with his 'Wild Garden' and 'Wild Lawn' ideas, spurned the shears for a more natural look. Writing in *Garden Design* in 1892, he quoted with loathing an author called Sedding, a man who urged the art of 'vegetable sculpture' on the British public. Here is Sedding in full flight:

" I have no more scruple on using the scissors on tree or shrub, where trimness is desirable, than I have in mowing the turf of the lawn that once represented a virgin world. There is a quaint charm in the results of the topiary art, in the prim imagery of evergreens, that all ages have felt. And I would even introduce bizarreries on the principle of not leaving all that is wild and odd to Nature outside of the garden paling ... "

The shear-mad Sedding went further, as you would expect of somebody who equates a mown lawn and a 'virgin world'. He later listed pyramids, peacocks, cocked hats and even 'ramping lions in Lincoln green' as topics that met with his full approval. The other side of the nineteenth century lawn craze was that it extended to gardens and gardening, and topiary was just a part of it, though the aim was always to provide drama on the lawn, and to have fun doing it. Fun came first. Always.

LAWN GAMES

The nobility in their palaces and stately homes appreciated the pleasures of well cropped lawns, though they felt no need to limit the lawns' size. Their sweat did not drizzle down their backs as they swung the scythe, heaved the roller, or hauled the water cart on hot, dry, dusty drought-ridden days. That was done by menials. Later lawn owners did sweat, however. In two ways.

First, they competed to produce the best lawn. Second, once lawn games such as badminton, croquet and bowls arose as codified forms of more ancient pursuits, people began to compete *on* the lawn as well as *with* the lawn. These lawn games all seem to have originated in Europe and travelled to North America, Australia, and various pockets of the British Empire.

The height of lawn gamery was probably reached on a Saturday in July 1923. On that day, the owner of *The Times*, Major the Hon. J.J. Astor, MP, and Lady Violet Astor, opened up their home, Hever Castle, Kent (once the childhood home of Anne Boleyn) to the entire staff of all departments of *The Times* and *The Times* Book Club and their wives and relatives, who were invited to enjoy themselves on the lawns 'in the cool shade of the great trees'.

The employees arrived on special trains and were served lunch in a large marquee before being set loose to stroll the grounds, admiring the statuary, topiary and 'lawns extending to the edge of the lake'. There were shooting contests on the Hever range, and there were keenly fought lawn tennis and golf matches. 'An amusing feature of the day was a baby show, specially arranged for those mothers who preferred to bring their babies with them, rather than leave them at home'.

Within a few years, that would change. A stock market crash, the ensuing depression and the war that followed would end an era when the rich, and even the moderately well-off, had domestic servants to free them up for amusements on the lawn, a time when plays featured young men bounding in through French windows crying 'I say! Anyone for tennis?'

There is doubt about when modern lawn tennis was developed. According to Colonel W.M. Playfair, writing to *The Times* in 1927, he witnessed the invention of tennis at Naini Tal in India, in 1871, by a Major Wingfield.

Others would take the origins of the game all the way back to the Elizabethan era. When Queen Elizabeth I visited Elvetham in Hampshire in 1591, her host was the Earl of Hertford. The standard procedure for a royal visit was to organise a hunt, but Elvetham was only a couple of miles across, too small to support hunting, so the Earl dammed a small river to form a lake with three islands, one of them decorated with topiary.

> " ... ten of the Earle's ... servants ... in a square greene court, before Her Majestie's windowe, did hang up lines, squaring out the forme of a tennis-court, and making a crosse-line in the middle. In this square ... They played, five to five, with the hand-ball at bord and cord (as they tearme it). "

The expression 'bord and cord' sounds like a reference to a primitive tennis racquet, but it could equally be a Japanese koto, or a precursor to badminton, if you want to push the boundaries a bit. Whatever it was, it seems to be quite unlike 'real tennis', which was played on an indoor court. The main point is that there were games, played with a ball on a grass court, long before lawn tennis. It was an idea waiting to emerge, once the right lawn conditions were available.

Almost as the *Silens Messor* came on the market, lawn games began to emerge, but it quickly became more than just garden games. Clubs and societies formed, rules were drawn up and competitions started. The 1850s and 1860s were the years when many games became popular and organised. Some of the new sports just had to be found, not invented. Normal hockey, the game played on grass, was around in the 1500s, but the first written rules were set down in the 1860s.

A small caveat: if the lawn mower made a range of new sports possible, there was some other influence out there as well, promoting the pursuit of novel and unusual sports around the period 1855 to 1865. It probably related to Britain's pride in its empire, but it showed up in the Latin tag *mens sana in corpore sano*, meaning a healthy mind in a healthy body. Whatever the driving force was, the new lawns granted by the lawn mower seemed perfect for sport, but there were other sports emerging, away from the lawn in that decade. The earliest recorded game of ice hockey may have been in 1859, and Edward Whymper visited the Alps in 1860, and became the first serious sporting climber.

The British army had used 'Indian club' exercises in the early nineteenth century, the first book on exercising with the clubs was published in Britain in 1834. Then in 1862, Sim D. Kehoe began making the clubs in New York, after seeing them in Britain in 1861. When he published *Indian Club Exercise* in 1866, he triggered the 'Physical Culture Movement' around the world, but it was most popular in Europe and North America.

FROM ETON TO WIMBLEDON

The Duke of Wellington is often quoted as saying that 'the battle of Waterloo was won on the playing fields of Eton'. When he was a student there in the 1780s, there were no playing fields. The Duke had died in 1852, but a Frenchman, the Comte d'Alembert, gave the first version of the 'quote', with a rather different wording, in 1855. It was then repeated by Sir Edward Creasy in *Eminent Etonians*, but the version we know today first appeared in print in 1889 by Sir William Fraser. The Iron Duke, by the way, was a mediocre scholar who detested his time at Eton, and was unlikely to credit Eton with anything.

Before about 1855, superior Britons saw sport as hunting, shooting and fishing, but by 1860, all true Britons believed in turning boys into men through games with maximal violence and close contact with grass and mud. The origins of the tradition of 'a healthy mind in a healthy body' (which sounds grander in Latin as *mens sana in corpore sano*) appear to be lost. Most authors just call it 'mid-Victorian', but if I had to hazard a guess about when it started, I would go for 1857, the year that *Tom Brown's School Days* and Charles Kingsley's *Two Years Ago* came out. Kingsley, soon to become chaplain to Queen Victoria, used the phrase 'muscular Christianity' in his book.

The golden year for the emergence of sports has to be 1859, with a new sporting enthusiasm showing up all over the world. That year, the rules of Australian Rules football were drafted. In India, the Maharajah of Manipur formed the first polo club, though it was called a horse hockey club at first, and only took the name 'polo', a Balti word for a wooden ball, later.

THE whole world, of course, has gnomes, but it seems that North America is the last home of the lawn deer. This choice of lawn ornamentation can occasionally be a problem. In one case, confirmed by the lovely people at snopes.com, a family in Waterboro, Maine, had a fake deer made of plastic foam on their lawn. This was both an ornament and an archery target. Regrettably, it was sufficiently life-like to attract the attentions of an amorous bull moose estimated at 700 pounds (320 kg).

Lonely bulls may pursue dairy cows or even woo inanimate objects. In this case, the bull only lost interest when the fake deer's head fell off, though the earlier loss of the antlers had been no discouragement at all. Perhaps there is something to be said for having a dummy deer on the lawn, to draw the moose's attentions away from you.

By the 1860s, people had plenty of games to play on lawn, but croquet seems to have been the leader. It came to England from Ireland in the early 1850s (though a variant was played by Languedoc peasants in the 1300s). From England, it then transferred to both Australia and the USA and took off in the 1860s. Soon the croquet lawn was considered an essential possession for the civilised family.

We will return to croquet, but before croquet could even become established, there was a spin-off. The first experimental game of lawn tennis was played on a croquet lawn in 1859. A solicitor named Major Thomas Henry Gem and his friend Batista Pereira, a Spanish merchant, were living in Birmingham, England. They tried a game that they loosely termed 'pelota' after a Spanish ball game. Soon after, it came to be known as lawn tennis. They began playing in earnest in 1860. In 1874 they formed the Leamington Tennis Club, which laid out the rules of the game.

The tennis-croquet link remained, and the All England Croquet Club was formed in 1868 to provide an official body to control the game and unify the laws. The club's members leased four acres (1.7 hectares) at Wimbledon the next year. Tennis courts were only added later when interest in croquet waned. Keeping up with the times, the club changed its name in 1899 to the All England Lawn Tennis and Croquet Club, and this has been its name to the present day, though most of us think of it only as 'Wimbledon'.

The game of 'Battledore and Shuttlecock' was probably developed in ancient Greece, and it survived in all sorts of odd corners of the world. It resurfaced in the nineteenth century and featured in an 1854 cartoon in *Punch*. In the 1860s, badminton began in India, a formalised version of the game incorporating a net. The rules were written down in 1877, but by then it was a popular lawn game in England. There were also a variety of other games that never really took off, often based on traditional regional English games like 'lawn billiards'.

The first 'British Open' (as golfers outside Britain know The Open Championship) was played in 1860. The first Melbourne Cup, still one of the great horse races in the world, was run in 1861, the Football Association was formed in Britain in 1863 (the first inter-club match of football, the game known to some heathens as 'soccer', was played at the end of 1860). The Rugby Football Union was formed in 1870.

These sports seem all to have arisen after the creation of new fields for play that could now be mown on a regular basis, letting players run swiftly over them, allowing balls to carry, rather than pulling up dead. It would be impolite of me to discuss in detail the problems faced (as it were) by players in tackles and rucks on a pitch strewn with cowpats, but the reader can probably join the dots.

There were about 6000 cricketers within 100 miles of New York in 1859, but the end of cricket as a popular sport in the US was near. From New Orleans to Massachusetts, there was an upswing of interest in baseball that saw cricket almost disappear from American turf. Even in late 1864, the *New York Times* reported on the publication, just in time for Christmas, of *The American Boy's Book of Sports and Games*, which outlined games to be played in the playground or outdoors with '... Toys, Marbles, Tops, Hoops, Kites, Archery, Balls, with Cricket, Croquet and Base Ball'.

Depending on the binding, parents could outlay US$3.50 or US$4.00 to obtain the work, with nearly 700 engravings on 600 pages, instructing the young on ways to 'relieve the tedium of leisure hours', as well as assorted athletic pursuits, amusements with pets, magic tricks and more. Note that it was American boys who were the target of the book, and it was boys who played most of the lawn-based games.

Croquet was an exception to this gender bias, a game that let women begin to play on the lawn. Three days before Christmas 1864, the *New York Times* offered up some ideas for desperate parents, including '... the famous croquet game, about which all England seems to be running mad, and the invention of which seems to have been suggested by the experience of John Bull running our blockade'. (This was during the US Civil War, when Confederate ports were blockaded by the Union, but neutral British ships still tried to trade.)

Against this explanation, the earliest record of croquet in America is from 1859. Then in 1865, at the end of the Civil War, the Newport Croquet Club was formed in Rhode Island. During a baseball match between 'The Atlantic Nine' against a combined New York–New Jersey team at the end of 1865, 'a party of ladies occupied the lower portion of the field, and had an interesting match at croquet', a spectacle which was, according to the *New York Times*, more interesting to several hundreds of those present than the baseball match.

In the post-Civil War, post-Lincoln period, Mrs Harriet Beecher Stowe, perhaps better known as the author of *Uncle Tom's Cabin*, commented in *The Atlantic Monthly* in 1866:

> **Croquet parties, which bring young people together by daylight for a healthy exercise, and end with a moderate share of the evening, are a very desirable amusement. What are called 'lawn teas' are finding great favor in England and some parts of our country. They are simply an early tea enjoyed in a sort of picnic style in the grounds about the house. Such an entertainment enables one to receive a great many at a time, without crowding, and, being in its very idea rustic and informal, can be arranged with very little expense or trouble. With the addition of lanterns in the trees and a little music, this entertainment may be carried on far into the evening with a very pretty effect.**

Even Alice played croquet when she visited the Queen of Hearts in Wonderland. They played on a croquet ground that '... was all ridges and furrows; the balls were live hedgehogs, the mallets live flamingos, and the soldiers had to double themselves up and to stand on their hands and feet, to make the arches', so perhaps calling it a lawn might have been seen as a bit of a stretch.

The game could also be associated with violence. In August 1866, a Mr and Mrs Smith of Chicago beat a burglar with their croquet mallets. Mr Smith accidentally landed a blow on Mrs Smith, during the melée, while she smashed several panes of glass with badly aimed attempts at hitting the burglar. After Mr Smith had kicked the senseless villain a few times, they ejected him from the house, and according to the *Chicago Tribune*, he died during the night. Less than three weeks later, the paper ran a story headed 'The Romance of Croquet', but in later issues, there is no hint of the fate of the Smiths. We must assume that they were acclaimed rather than punished for their act.

Croquet travelled to Australia just as rapidly. It was mentioned in advertisements in the Tasmanian *Walch's Literal Intelligencer* in 1861. Advertisements for croquet equipment became common in Queensland papers around 1862, and there are photographs of people playing at Government House in Perth in about 1863.

By August 1863, a Brisbane paper complained that Post Office staff had gone off to Moreton Island on a Saturday afternoon 'with a party of fair enslavers to play croquet', rather than sorting the mails. Two months later and on the other side of Australia, a Perth newspaper complained that croquet players in the Perth Public Garden might harm the 'beautiful grass plots' after so many years' attention had been lavished on the present fine sward.

The January 1871 issue of *Scribner's Monthly* features a reference to indoor croquet sets as Christmas gifts, but by 1872, the lawn was sufficiently common that *Scribner's* saw fit to carry no less than three articles in 'Home and Society' on the finer points of croquet, from the best timbers to make mallets and balls to striking methods such as the sledge-hammer and the spoony. The sledge-hammer style was described as best suited to slaying oxen, while the spoony style was denigrated as one '... by which some old Betty in pantaloons secures accuracy of stroke at the sacrifice of all elegance and grace'.

In 1873, the *New York Times* used the nation's continuing enthusiasm for croquet to show how plain were the circumstances of a Free Methodist camp meeting in Dover, New Jersey, by explaining that there were '... no smooth-shaven lawns upon which charming young ladies can kill the slowly passing time at croquet....'.

In October 1874, *Manufacturer and Builder* offered a plan for a house which could be completed for US$3500. Included in the front view was a broad vista of lawn on which a gentleman and two ladies played croquet, but not everybody saw croquet as a marker or maker of civilisation.

There was, asserted *Scribner's Monthly* in 1874, 'no one sport where well-bred people are apt to approach so near to ill-breeding, as on the Croquet-ground'. The cause of the trouble, said the writer, appeared to be differences in players' understanding of the rules, which were far from standard. Girls went almost into hysterics and young men became sullen and disputatious over a game intended solely for amusement.

A conference of English croquet clubs in January 1870 had adopted a code of laws which was later revised by the votes of the clubs, so that there was solid agreement. In the US, where croquet was less formally organised, there was little reason why US players would ever agree on a single binding rule book. This made a wholesale adoption of the English rules attractive, said 'Uncle Charley'. Then as the 1870s wound down, fashions shifted, aided and abetted by Maurice Thompson. In 1877, he had a two-page article in *Scribner's Monthly*. The subject was 'Bow Shooting', and he wrote:

> **Archery clubs of from seven to fifteen members, both ladies and gentlemen, could be formed all over the country more easily, at less expense, and with far better results than cricket, croquet, or base-ball clubs.**

By May 1878, Thompson raised the stakes, trumpeting the joys of archery in a 16-page piece, 'Merry Days with Bow and Quiver' in *Scribner's Monthly*.

> I wish to press advantages over croquet, badminton, lawn-tennis, and all like games. First, it requires no stooping, which, for ladies, is a deleterious thing to health, as it tends to compress the vital organs and to interfere with digestion and the circulation of the blood. In shooting, you stand erect and every motion tends to expand the chest and stimulate the vital centers by promoting free circulation of the blood, and deep, healthful respiration. This, in the pure air of the country or sea-side, is the best possible medicine for persons whose delicate chests give warning of pulmonic weakness.

Thompson's book, *The Witchery of Archery*, was reviewed favourably in *The Atlantic Monthly* in August 1879. Said the reviewer:

> **Now that archery seems about to displace croquet in the hearts and on the lawns of summer pleasurers,**

we know no greater favor we can do them than to direct them to Mr Thompson's manual for both the literature and the practice of their graceful sport. 99

In the same month, *Scribner's* declared lawn tennis to be the new rage in America. It was athletic but not too violent, able to be played by women and children and just needed 'four or more bats and balls, two poles, a net twenty six feet by five feet; two guy ropes with runners and pegs and a mallet'. They forgot the lawn mower, or perhaps they just took it for granted that their readers would own one—and a roller.

In 1883, an advertisement in the *Washington Post* offered books on a range of outdoor sports including lawn pool, lawn tennis, archery and croquet. So croquet was still holding on, but its end as a mainstream sport was surely in sight. The rise of baseball and other spectator sports, the growing popularity of golf and other distractions called people away— and in some daring places, women joined the men in going on picnics!

THE RISE OF THE PICNIC

There were even bigger changes on the way, because the late 1850s were also a time of great parks. As we have seen, New York's Central Park opened to the public in 1859, though in London, in the same year, the Vauxhall Gardens closed to the public, to the great pleasure of moralists of all colours. Still, with growing expanses of mown public grass, the picnic came into vogue.

The original picnics were probably French, but their sort of *pique nique* seems to have been an indoor meal of the pot luck variety, one of those gatherings where everybody brought something. The outdoor picnic probably owed its origin to the removal of animal mowers from the grass, and that had to wait on the arrival and popularisation of the mechanical lawn mower.

The *Oxford English Dictionary* reports that 'picnic' appeared in print in English in 1748, but the idea boomed just when the lawn did. In 1861, Mrs Beeton, the author of *Household Management* provided a list of the necessities for a picnic of 40 people.

Once sheep (or even worse, cattle) ceased to be the main form of lawn mower, ladies and gentlemen in fine garb might risk being seated upon the ground, though it remained preferable to have some sort of waterproof or water resistant cloth, because not all grass was lawn. Drainage was often poor and the fen was muddier than the sward.

London's Hyde Park was less than ideal as a picnic place in 1851. *The Times* complained of filth and detritus 'among which dirty bits of newspaper, stale orange peel, bones, rags and other rubbish are prominently visible; neither is it at all agreeable, however fond one may be of horses, to nose all the concentrated ammonia from the Knightsbridge barracks'.

In the twenty-first century, we have forgotten the realities that led Trinculo in *The Tempest* to exclaim to Caliban: 'Monster, I do smell all horse-piss, at which my nose is in great indignation', but the copious micturition of horses was a reality in the mid-nineteenth century, and even more alarming at a time when people believed that strong odours and miasmatic vapours caused disease. *The Times* advised its readers to wear double-soled boots.

One picnic in somewhat moist surroundings came close to provoking a riot, and it certainly caused many vapours. It wasn't real, but a painting, executed in 1863 by Edouard Manet, *Le déjeuner sur l'herbe*. It shows two fully clothed men, a naked woman, and one bathing, apparently in some form of chemise of limited opacity. The naked woman has the face of one of his favourite models, but the body is that of his wife. Perhaps he hoped in this way to mollify the prudes, but it didn't wash, even if the work was originally called *Le Bain* (The Bath).

There are curious contradictions: the man on the right wears a hat that would normally be worn indoors, and even if this is 'Luncheon on the Grass', the surface is less than lawn-like. In 1865, Monet executed a painting with the same name, but this showed a larger party, all fully clothed, and with a formal cloth laid on the ground. This was more what the middle classes desired, with less of the green and bare it, thank you very much.

The sweeping dresses of the ladies in that era would have swept up more than they had bargained for in a field frequented by cows. That said, many years ago, a very old lady described to me her habit, with 'her young man' of going into a cow pasture and rudely shoving a lying cow out of the way, so as to obtain a drier and warmer piece of ground. Obviously, cows were not entirely a bad thing to have around, if you watched your step. Her recollections probably dated from the 1880s or 1890s.

Parks with their pleasant lawns could sometimes become the focus of riots: in 1855, London's Hyde Park was the scene of a riot as Londoners protested the Sunday Trading Bill, which forbade any buying or selling on what was, for most people, their only day off work. In 1866, the same park was the site of a major riot as protesters marched, assembled and speechified, all without the blessing of the police. When they were refused access to Hyde Park, they tore down the park railings and entered without permission, terrifying the middle classes. Still, the very next year, a major Reform Bill was passed, extending the vote to more of the English population.

Most picnics, like those in Hyde Park (and other London parks) in 1916, were more sedate. War had prevented people taking an August break at Margate, Eastbourne, Harrogate or Scotland, and so they took their luncheons in baskets, or reviving an eighteenth century style, shared an open-air breakfast. Some of them might feed on the grass, others took to boats. In the distance, reported *The Times*, catering to a hunger for the pastoral, those in Kensington Gardens might see distant sheep and lambs.

Open air and the outdoors were commonly seen as healthy, and in a time when tuberculosis was rife, and often spread under crowded indoor conditions, in an age when rickets was still common in children who got too little sunlight to drive the manufacture of vitamin D, perhaps that was so.

THE RISE AND FALL OF THE PROFESSIONAL LAWN

✳ ✳ ✳

An amateur could still make his own lawn tennis court in the 1930s, but who would bother today? Reginald Beale advised the lawn maker to sow 1 to 4 ounces of seed per square yard (30 to 130 grams per square metre), adding that if the surface was to be used for tennis, there should be no false economies. The owner had to mark up a yard grid, sow the seed, then rake it in to a depth of half an inch, before rolling the surface lightly. Choose a dry day, Beale advised, a day when the soil does not stick to the boots or roller.

For the most part, the establishment, maintenance, upkeep and repair of sporting sites was left to professionals, with perhaps the exception of a few home tennis and croquet grounds, and the occasional home putting green. By the twentieth century, golf venues were most definitely becoming more genteel, with professionals caring for them.

In Britain, old hands mourned the replacement of golf links where wilderness might abound. The rot began in 1820, when Alexander Monroe accepted £4 a year to maintain the Aberdeen golf links and to keep the holes in good order. By 1900, the well-off let the greenkeepers take over the cares of lawn management. The final decline from golf links to golf course can be seen in a court case from Wales.

In 1910, Britain's High Court heard a case on appeal from the Abergavenny County Court. A group of gentlemen had, in 1899, obtained a lease to an established clubhouse and a licence to make and maintain a golf course on the nearby farming land, which was used as pasture. Covenants on the lease allowed them to maintain a playing course, 50 yards wide, which would be clear of long grass and ferns. Then in 1905, the owner let the grazing to a Mr Woodward, with the golf course provision as part of the lease. At first, Woodward's sheep and cattle kept the grass down and all was well.

In 1906, the golf club began using a scythe, and in 1907, brought in a horse-drawn mowing machine. Woodward complained that they were taking his grass and brought an action claiming damages for trespass, which the

County Court rejected. On appeal, the High Court confirmed the verdict. The judges gave Woodward leave to appeal further, though he appears not to have done so.

The central issue was how long grass could be before it was judged to be 'long grass'. The original lease did not specify this, but the exacting demands of the gentlemen golfers led to the mowing machine being set so low as to leave only half to three quarters of an inch (12 to 18 mm) of grass.

The appellant argued for an application of an 1899 standard for what constituted a playable course, the defendant (the golf club) argued that 'long grass' should be defined, not from the point of view of a sheep seeking a meal, but from that of a golfer. In other words, grass which was too long to allow golf in accordance with a reasonable standard was long grass, and this was the basis of the judgment. Golf had ceased to be a game for the hairy-chested, and had become a game for the effete.

In 1920, as Britain got itself up and running after World War I, golfers emerged to express their concerns. Older golfers fumed that golf links were now mere golf courses. Herbert Maxwell pointed out in the pages of *The Times* that links were defined as 'sandy flat ground on the seashore', and on those, the bunkers remained as the sea winds shaped them. In the good old days, golf architects were unheard-of, and greens were natural patches of close sward, requiring no attention other than the sweeping-off of worm casts. Now, said Maxwell, the putting green of the modern game was as spacious as a croquet lawn.

Perhaps there was no way of illustrating this better, he said, than by quoting the 1777 decree from the council of the Royal and Ancient Club to the effect that players were to tee their balls from a point between one and four club lengths from the previous hole. He added that this rule remained in force in 1855 when George Glennie, using a feather ball and long-headed clubs, completed 18 holes in 88 strokes, a score which remained a course record until 1884.

More golfers spent more of their time at the 19th hole. Talking and reading about games, along with watching others play them, began to be regarded as the equivalent of actually taking part.

SPECTATOR SPORTS

This new dedication to talking and reading about games explains why a lawn-equipped sport-loving world was ready for the official first modern Olympics in 1896. In 1898, journalists were starting to look at their century and describe the fashions they could see. *The Spectator* explored this in an article called 'Fashions in pastimes', which was reproduced in *The Living Age* in September.

66 Most people deemed [croquet] dead beyond redemption, when it was all the while cultivated by an esoteric coterie of enthusiasts, and within the last few years it has emerged from obscurity to such good purpose as to compete effectively with the very game which apparently gave it its death-blow—lawn-tennis. The fluctuations of lawn-tennis, again, are in their way quite as remarkable. For a while it carried all before it. Everybody played the game, and the fact that it was practically the first active pastime in which the two sexes freely participated lent it an immense social prestige. Then gradually it fell into the hands of specialists, and is now cultivated mainly by experts, the recent championship meeting at Wimbledon attracting an audience curiously

**unlike that which used to assemble in the days of
the Renshaws. 99**

We can see early intimations here of spectator sport, and the writer could
see them as well, but he could also see the influences of his fellow scribes,
the forerunners of today's commentators and announcers. As the players
became more professional, so did the writers and talkers who moulded the
public's thoughts.

> **66 If base-ball had been championed by so graceful
> and convincing a pen as that of Mr Horace Hutchinson,
> or cultivated by so interesting a personage as Mr Balfour,
> it might have emerged from the stage of exotic existence
> which it still leads on our shores. The leading tendency
> in modern pastime is to develop its spectacular aspect,
> mainly, if not entirely, from commercial motives. 99**

Horace Hutchinson (1859–1932) was the golf columnist and editor of
Country Life, and so popularised the sport. 'Mr Balfour' was probably Arthur
Balfour, the future British Prime Minister, best known today for the 'Balfour
Declaration'. In 1898, he was the Leader of the House of Commons and a
shrewd political operator whose golf writing was still one of his greater
claims to fame.

Notice the suggestions in this next excerpt from the *Living Age* article,
implying that modern professional spectator sports are of the same family
as gladiatorial contests, and that they pursue the spectacular in preference
to healthier activities.

> **66 Over a great part of the Midlands and the North
> of England amateur football has been submerged by
> professionalism, and the clubs are financed by small
> syndicates, who engage players—generally from across the
> Border—and recoup themselves by the takings at the 'gate'.
> Hence the anomaly of a football team named after the town
> for which they play, but not containing a single local player.**

SILBER & FLEMING'S LAWN TENNIS GOODS.

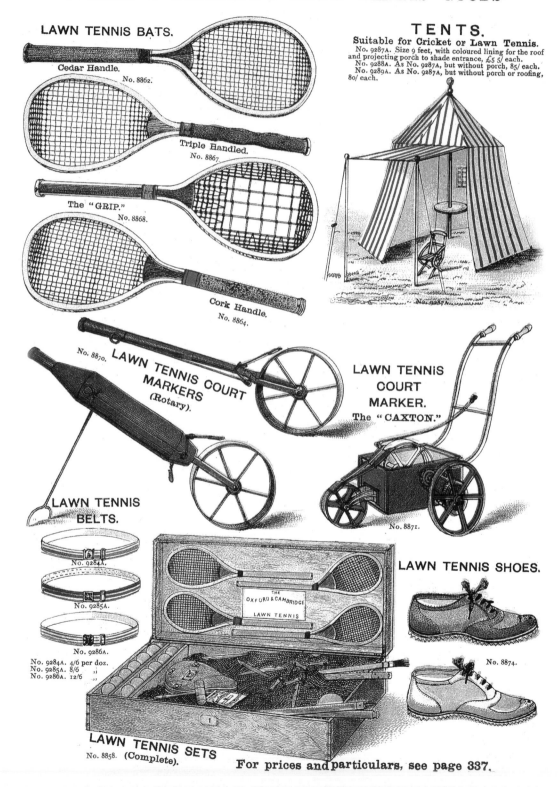

LAWN TENNIS BATS.

Cedar Handle.
No. 8862.

Triple Handled.
No. 8867.

The "GRIP."
No. 8868.

Cork Handle.
No. 8864.

TENTS.

Suitable for Cricket or Lawn Tennis.

No. 9287A. Size 9 feet, with coloured lining for the roof and projecting porch to shade entrance, £5 5/ each.
No. 9288A. As No. 9287A, but without porch, 85/ each.
No. 9289A. As No. 9287A, but without porch or roofing, 80/ each.

No. 9287A.

LAWN TENNIS COURT MARKERS
(Rotary).

No. 8870.

LAWN TENNIS COURT MARKER.
The "CAXTON."

No. 8871.

LAWN TENNIS BELTS.

No. 9284A.
No. 9285A.
No. 9286A.

No. 9284A. 4/6 per doz.
No. 9285A. 8/6 ,,
No. 9286A. 12/6 ,,

THE
OXFORD & CAMBRIDGE
LAWN TENNIS

LAWN TENNIS SHOES.

No. 8874.

LAWN TENNIS SETS
No. 8858. (Complete).

For prices and particulars, see page 337.

These inter-club matches are witnessed by enormous crowds—ten thousand being quite an ordinary number—including most of the able-bodied youth of the neighborhood, who apparently prefer the Continental practice of hiring athletes to make sport for them to the older method of playing games themselves.

Professional football, in fact, approximates more closely than any other institution, save that of the bull-ring, to the gladiatorial games of Imperial Rome. It is certainly exciting to watch, but it involves a great expenditure of money, encourages loafing, drinking and betting amongst the spectators, and develops in the football gladiator himself qualities which, to put it mildly, do not conduce to domestic happiness. 99

But even if most of the popular games were developed around 1860, there were those casting around for novel spectacles to offer the masses. One mooted possibility was '... the introduction of the famous Basque game of pelota, because of its great spectacular possibilities'. This was not on, thought the writer:

66 Now, pelota is undoubtedly a splendid game, as the most patriotic Britishers have reluctantly admitted; but it is so arduous and exhausting that for practical purposes it can only be played by highly trained experts of great strength or endurance—the Basques are men of marvellous physique—who for the rest are notorious for 'selling' their matches.

No, we have plenty of games, and plenty of professionalism, with all its attendant evils, without importing pelota. 99

What would the writer have thought of the payments made to 'sporting personalities' today? A lot of people have accepted the obscene payouts made to the stars and can be persuaded to believe almost anything, though even the truth is fairly amazing. In 2004, golfer Tiger Woods was reported to have paid US$20 million for a 155-foot yacht, which he named *Privacy*. He later filed a privacy-rights lawsuit against the yacht's builders, because they had used his name and image to advertise their products without permission. He reportedly gained a satisfactory settlement.

That incident, or something else, inspired a joker, or more probably two jokers, to touch up a picture of an aircraft carrier, but it was done in two stages. The first part had the flight deck covered in grass with a single golf hole and a 'clubhouse', the second added a golfer figure and the name 'Tiger' across the bows. In that form, it can be found on the internet to this day, circulating as one of those 'can you believe this?' items.

No, if you are wondering, you *can't* believe it. Very few grasses are tough enough to stand up to that level of exposure to the salt spray that blows over every ocean-going ship. Mind you, if you were willing to drive your tee shot over the clubhouse, a decent aircraft carrier, at 300 to 340 metres would be long enough for a shortish par 4 hole with ferocious water hazards.

THE COROLLARIES OF A SPORTING CRAZE

Sport had followed the lawn mower, spreading out over the smooth surfaces. Before long, people demanded that the domestic lawn become a safer surface, a true and level field on which to compete. Then having followed the mower, sport drove the lawnless to join the ranks of the lawned, but it also drove a demand for more playing fields, all covered in grass. Private grass inspired demands for more public grass.

Today, the different grass surfaces have led to a proliferation of sports shoes, designed to take into account the different surfaces, the traction and skidding, the torque and twisting that comes from a particular grass (or synthetic) surface.

Sadly, not everybody appreciates sport. Some people dislike lawyers in much the same way, but I find Lord Denning's views on cricket a delight to read. Denning was not your average lawyer. He was an erudite and witty mathematician, barrister and judge who retired in 1982 at the age of 83, as a widely-admired Master of the Rolls.

This brings us to Miller v. Jackson, also known as 'The Cricket Case'. Denning's dissenting judgement when it went to appeal has pleased law students ever since, but it deserves to please a wider audience. The case involved a Mr and Mrs Miller who tired of having cricket balls hit into their garden and against their house, and the local cricket club. For non-cricketers, when the ball clears the boundary on the full, that is 'a six', and six runs are added to the total of the batting side.

Cricket balls are rather like baseballs in size and weight. They are hard, and potentially deadly. The Millers' house adjoined a long-established cricket field, so sooner or later more balls would fall. The cricket field existed when they bought the house, but the Millers sought damages and an order to stop the local club-playing cricket on the field. Denning opened his dissenting judgement like this:

> **" In summertime village cricket is the delight of everyone. Nearly every village has its own cricket field where the young men play and the old men watch. In the village of Lintz in County Durham they have their own ground, where they have played these last 70 years. They tend it well. The wicket area is well rolled and mown. The outfield is kept short. It has a good club house for the players and seats for the onlookers. The village team play there on Saturdays and Sundays. They belong to a league, competing with the neighbouring villages. On other evenings after work they practise while the light lasts. Yet now after these 70 years a judge of the High Court has ordered that they must not play there any more. He has issued an injunction to stop them. He has done it at the instance of a newcomer who is no lover of cricket. This newcomer has built, or has had built for him, a house on the edge of the cricket ground which four years ago was a field where cattle grazed. The animals did not mind the cricket. But now this adjoining field has been turned into a housing estate. The newcomer bought one of the houses on the edge of the cricket ground. No doubt the**

open space was a selling point. Now he complains that when a batsman hits a six the ball has been known to land in his garden or on or near his house. His wife has got so upset about it that they always go out at week-ends. They do not go into the garden when cricket is being played. They say that this is intolerable. So they asked the judge to stop the cricket being played. And the judge, much against his will, has felt that he must order the cricket to be stopped: with the consequence, I suppose, that the Lintz Cricket Club will disappear. The cricket ground will be turned to some other use. I expect for more houses or a factory. The young men will turn to other things instead of cricket. The whole village will be much the poorer. And all this because of a newcomer who has just bought a house there next to the cricket ground. 🙶

Think how legal proceedings might have been enlivened in the US if cricket had been retained there as well! And that is even when you leave out the risk of injury. Oddly enough, a cricket injury may have changed the history of the USA.

In March of 1751, Frederick Lewis, Prince of Wales, (and the father of King George III), died as the result of an internal abscess. This developed as the result of a blow that he took from a cricket ball some months earlier, when he was playing on the lawn of Cliefden House, in Buckinghamshire.

This put a young King George III on the throne when his grandfather, George II, died in 1760. If he had been forced to wait until the end of his father's reign, his infirmities might have been noted, and something might have been done to bypass him, but once his tailbone hit the throne, he was harder to dislodge. Perhaps, just perhaps, when cricket on the lawn placed a dotty king on the throne, that sealed the future of the USA. Somehow, I think a British King Fred would at best have only delayed the inevitable, but it is nice to wonder about.

In 2002, I walked along the Mall in Washington DC, another of Downing's designs. I was there in part to cover a geophysics conference, but I was also researching a book and that took me to the various Smithsonian venues. As I

IN Canada, where accurate figures have been taken and genuine estimates made, each year sees all sorts of lawn mowers emit almost 272 to 413 tons of nitrogen oxides, 9649 to 12,762 tons of hydrocarbons, 67 to 86 thousand tons of carbon monoxide and 275 to 414 thousand tons of particulates. While carbon dioxide emissions are not given, fuel consumption is estimated at 110 to 144 million tons, which would generate between 350 and 450 million tons of CO_2. If you converted that to dry ice, you would have a cube 800 metres (half a mile) along each edge, just from lawn mowers in Canada!

crossed the Mall, I saw that I was walking over a cricket pitch. It must have been set up for expatriates from Australasia, Britain or the Indian sub-continent, but while I kept an eye on it over the next week, I never saw it in use. Five years later, I went back and looked for it again, but it had gone. Perhaps it was deemed too dangerous to play cricket on the mall that Downing had constructed.

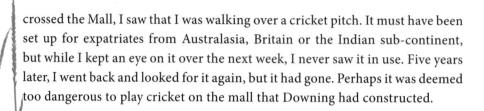

LAWN'S FUTURE

As we have seen, the cost of lawns is huge, but there is more to the story. It is not only the straightforward dollar cost, but a variety of other costs as well: excessive use of water, pollution caused by fertiliser and spray runoffs, as well as the various wastes generated by an obsessive demand for tidiness.

The Book of Isaiah has been the inspiration, either directly or indirectly for many who dreamed of making the desert bloom. It is foretold that the desert will bloom when the Messiah comes, so Mormons, Israelis and others have had the same dream; even early explorers in Australia expressed similar hopes. Indeed, in Australia, politicians and radio shock jocks still talk of turning coastal rivers inland, through, over or around mountain ranges to deliver water to the parched inland.

It matters little to the dreamers whether the desert in question is true desert or a suburban plot. In a strict sense, lawn is more of a desert, an area almost entirely devoid of biodiversity, but the lawn cultists don't see it that way. They drive the lawn to extremes, in a waste that is tragic when you consider the plight of people in drought-ridden Third World nations.

In the *Gardeners' Chronicle* in April 1853, 'CRD' (whom we now know to be Charles Robert Darwin) asked for advice on the use of canvas hose, coated and lined with gutta percha, as a siphon hose to move water from one tank to another. Watering at that time would usually have had to be carried out by watering can or bucket, and that was still so in Reginald Beale's time.

The English drought of 1929, Beale mourned, killed parts of his putting green, because he could not carry enough water the necessary hundred paces: by 1931, he had arranged to have pipes laid, and his hopes were high that he would never have such problems again. Watering in 1931 was mostly done with barrows and cans. Sprinklers, said Beale, were 'held in detestation by the water companies because they are so often turned on and forgotten, and in any case are very wasteful'.

THE COST OF LAWN

The grass grown in desert America and Australia, is watered at huge expense, then it is mowed, and the grass clippings are dumped. 'I am rich,' these lawns tell the world, 'so I can afford to waste the world's resources'. Water, won from distant mountains or pumped from deep underground is treated within an inch of its life, made good enough for quaffing with fine food, and then poured on the ground to soak in, run off or evaporate.

Petroleum feedstock is used to make hoses, fortunes are spent and greater fortunes won, digging the raw materials for plumbing out of the ground, so that pipes may be laid back in the ground, safe from the mower's blades. In a hot climate, between 50 and 70 per cent of the water coming onto a suburban property will go to watering lawns and gardens.

The EPA estimates that the value of lawn fertilisers derived from fossil fuels in the USA is more than US$5 billion a year. Much of this flows into groundwater or ends up in lakes, streams and rivers. There, it fuels a massive growth of algae that fall to the bottom where they rot, consuming all of the oxygen in the water and so creating 'dead zones' where nothing can live.

Before World War II, nitrogen fertilisers were spread at about one pound per thousand square feet, (around 3.5 kg/hectare). Just 25 years after the war, the common level in the USA was eight times as high. Each year, what fails to be washed into streams and lakes is swept up in lawn clippings that are taken and dumped. This is puzzling, because to those who took the time to notice, it was possible that the lawn could top-dress itself. As far back as 1859 (that year again!), Henry Winthrop Sargent updated Downing's book which is usually referred to as *Landscape Gardening*. In a supplement, Sargent wrote that except in May and June when the grass grows fastest, he had stopped using a 'box for catching the grass'. The wisdom was out there, but nobody noticed!

As our western societies move to double-income families with high-maintenance lifestyles, so people move more and more to the use of lawn care companies. In one study, the number of lawn care companies in Maine tripled between 1995 and 2001. Since labour costs are high, spraying is the easy way to go, so it comes as no surprise that the use of yard pesticides doubled over the same period.

On a larger scale, the EPA estimates that in the USA, 67,000,000 pounds, some 30,000 metric tons of synthetic pesticides, are used on US lawns each year, at a cost of around US$700,000,000. And each year, lawn mowers consume some 580 million gallons of gasoline (petrol)!

Some of the information provided is less than reliable. You can read that a lawn mower, operating for one hour, generates as much 'pollution' (a term that is never defined) as a car driving 350 miles (500 kilometres). In reality, it is more like the pollution generated by a car driving 20 miles (30 km): the figure is probably believed because few people spend an hour close-up behind their car with the engine running.

THE END OF AN ERA

As I penned the last words of the first draft, the Beijing Games of 2008 drew to an end in a spectacular ceremony with no lawn mowers on display, even though many of the world's mowers are now made in the People's Republic of China. The world's masses drifted away from their televisions, and worried about the world economy, an issue rather more serious than the bread, hooplas and circuses of the Games of the XXIX Olympiad.

A few months later, at the last revision, I had time to take stock. The Shanghai Stock Exchange was approaching its 18th birthday in free fall, but in all that time, no member of the politburo had been denounced for taking the capitalist road. In the USA on the other hand, President Bush had been swiftly denounced for 'socialism' for bailing out the US economy. His successor was equally rapidly accused of 'socialism' by his opponent (who lost), but the winner came across as a man of the people who might subscribe for magazines, who might even push the lawn-mower over the White House lawn in his shirt-sleeves of evenings—but who could be certain of anything?

Where will the future lie? Niels Bohr was right: the making of predictions is a difficult task, especially predictions about the future. Still, consider these pointers:

In Beijing, they stopped painting the street grass green. The Olympic turf on which the field athletics, the archery, the football (soccer), baseball and softball and maybe a few other sports had been played was replaced by durable artificial turf. The portable turf units in the main stadium had been carried in trays into the main arena after the opening ceremony, now they had gone out again. Droughts were causing concern in many countries, including Australia, Paraguay, Israel, parts of the USA, Afghanistan, Kenya, Somalia and North Korea.

In Toronto, people debated whether or not to replace the artificial turf that Toronto FC played on with natural grass. Elsewhere, the future seems to lie entirely with synthetic surfaces. These may be used as lawn, but they may not be lawn as we know it. Nonetheless, more and more lawn games are played on an imitation of grass that needs less water and fertiliser, no mowing and no weeding.

THE FUTURE OF LAWN

The path to Astroturf and its cousins started in the 1960s under another fresh-faced young president of the USA tried to introduce fitness and challenged Americans to travel 50 miles (80 km) in twenty hours. The First-World obesity epidemic, in large part supported by couch potatoes watching sport on television, was already under way.

In the past four decades, many more sports and sporting clubs have chosen synthetic surfaces. It began when the Ford Foundation concluded in the late 1950s that a lack of playing space made urban children less fit. The experts examined the medical records of US military intakes and compared urban and rural youths. The solution, they reported, was a resilient artificial surface, soft and giving like turf, but able to survive use all the year round, even in a city.

The first synthetic turf was Monsanto's Chemgrass. In 1966, the Houston Astrodome was an enclosed sporting arena where the grass died because, in simple terms, there was too little sunlight, once part of the clear roof had been painted to reduce glare inside. The solution was 'Astroturf'—Chemgrass with a new name. By the 1960s, Rachel Carson's campaigns had led to some distrust of 'chemicals', so it was probably a good move to rename it.

The original materials were polypropylene or nylon attached to a concrete or asphalt base. Admiral Cochrane—he who wanted to use asphalt as a 'manure'—would have been delighted to see a link, no matter how tenuous, between turf and asphalt! Other surfaces followed, not all of them successful in an era when television viewers demanded coverage and colour television could reveal problems, and problems there were.

The Orange Bowl in Florida acquired a Poly Turf surface which turned blue (not orange, which they might have been able to get away with, given the name). Poly Turf also melted in the hot Florida sun. Another field in Tennessee, turned black. More problems began to emerge: synthetic surfaces have a different 'give' to real turf, causing more falls and injuries. Some of the surfaces caused grazes and burns when players slid along them.

Research showed that synthetic surfaces were far cheaper for games like lawn bowls, but with a catch. The surfaces grew hotter in the sun, they became more slippery when they were wet, and the players, mostly elderly, would be hitting a far less forgiving surface if they slipped or fainted.

On the other hand, (field) hockey has moved in the past twenty years from a game played on a glorified tussocky cow paddock to one played on very fast synthetic turf. A very few of these have the gaps in the 'turf' filled with sand; most are 'water turf', where sprinklers operate between games and at half-time, in order to provide a better surface. The water that runs off can be collected and applied once more, so waste is minimised.

A hockey ball is identical in size and weight to a cricket ball, meaning it is very similar to a baseball, and it is hard. The ball moves fast across the surface, generally at a low altitude, though it can lift unpredictably on grass. There are many fewer injuries on water turf than on real grass. It is a spectacular game now, one well-suited to television.

Tennis is mainly played on synthetic surfaces or clay these days. For several years before the Beijing Olympics, Rafael Nadal was the supreme tennis player on clay, winning the French Open four times, while failing to beat Roger Federer on grass until the 2008 Wimbledon final, which he only won after an epic tussle. In May 2007, the two met in an exhibition match on a half-clay, half-grass court, where the usual 90-second end-change period was extended to two minutes, to allow the players time to change to the best footwear for each surface.

At the time, Federer had won 48 consecutive matches on grass while Nadal had taken 72 straight matches on clay. Using a split court, half grass, half clay, Nadal was the superior player on the day. Clay, though, was also a winner, because the grass end had to be replaced on the night before the game, when 'a plague of worms' damaged the original surface.

Between the attacks of the conservationists who point to the incredible waste that is lawn, the increased dollar and environmental costs in maintaining lawns and changing lifestyles which leave less time for lawnsmanship, it is possible that the traditional monoculture lawnscape may soon be a thing of the past. We simply cannot afford lawns any more.

THE FUTURE OF THE WORLD

Homes will be forced to have xeriscaped surfaces, areas designed to cope with local water and rain conditions, using natural grasses from the surrounding area that can live in the conditions found there. In some places, we may see grasses chosen more carefully, like the popular Australian cultivar of buffalo grass known as 'Sir Walter', a variety that is both shade- and drought-tolerant. We may also see more gravel 'lawns', more moss lawns and more lawns made of mint, thyme or other low plants.

If we don't, then we will see more deserts forming. Before, as or after that happens, we will see more wars fought over water. Wars over the water have been anticipated by conservationists and political analysts since the 1990s. Even without climate change, water in many parts of the world is in short supply, and what are people to think of their upstream neighbours who take precious water to maintain lawns?

In time, we may see the lawn mower become as rare as the scythe, but then again, perhaps we won't. Perhaps trying circumstances will lead to even more bread and circuses for the couch potatoes. Grass and our enthusiasm for it gave us the sports-mad world we live in, a world where everybody stops living to watch Olympic events for two weeks and talk of peace, before we go back to war.

Once, grass created many of the sports we play, but it seems that those sports have now left the grass behind. In the pursuit of spectacle and TV ratings for the sports that grass made, we have replaced grass with something insipid and lifeless, but that change may not be such a bad thing. Perhaps we have turned from grass just in time to save ourselves.

The post-Beijing world faces the prospect of global climate change with many more parts of the world under threat of drought. It faces the prospect of wars in the first half of the twenty-first century over access to water supplies. It faces a world where oil stocks are dwindling while demand and prices rise, a world where the squandering of scarce resources on grass and lawns makes less and less sense, where such perceived selfishness must lead to war.

By its nature, such a war would be one of scorched earth, sown salt, misery and devastation. Still, with some luck and a lot of good management, this is not an inevitable future. It remains a potential future, and when you look back at the ways lawn and the lawn mower changed our society, we would be unwise not to consider that they could change our world again.

And do the grasses have a future in this gloomy scenario? A few people may think it would be worthwhile for them to go extinct, so long as the moles, the earthworms, the rusts, the army worms and most importantly, the crabgrass and the kikuyu, go with us. A far larger number might be prepared to coexist with these and other neighbours.

I rather suspect that the crabgrass, the kikuyu and all their poaceous cousins have been reading Malvina Reynolds. They are biding their time. *God bless the grass!*

REFERENCES

Note: most of the nineteenth century American references were found using the Cornell University Making of America project. This applies in particular to articles from *Harper's New Monthly Magazine, Scribner's, Manufacturer and Builder. Living Age,* the *North American Review* and *Scientific American.* Articles from *The Times* were accessed online from the Thomson Gale Times Digital Archive, 1785–1985 through the State Library of NSW.

A.J.D., 'The Alpaca', letter to *The Times*, 21 August 1867.

Abel, Alan, *Yours For Decency*. London: Elek Books, 1967.

Aldersey-Williams, Hugh, 'Nature Mows Best', *New Statesman* 22 Aug. 1997: 42

Amero, Richard W., 'Samuel Parsons Finds Xanadu in San Diego', *The Journal of San Diego History*, Winter 1998, 44 (1). http://www.sandiegohistory.org/journal/98winter/parsons.htm, last accessed, September 1, 2008.

Anonymous, 'A Day at Hever', news report, *The Times*, 9 July 1923.

Anonymous, 'A Man Killed by a Mower', news report, *The Times*, 23 June 1858.

Anonymous, 'A suburban Home', *The Manufacturer and Builder*, April 1887, p. 92–3.

Anonymous, 'Agriculture as a Profession; or Hints about Farming', *New Englander and Yale Review*, 18 (issue 72), 899–908, November 1860.

Anonymous, 'Alternatives to Grass', article, *The Times*, 26 September 1942.

Anonymous, 'American Horticulture', *Atlantic Monthly*, April 1863, pp. 482–86.

Anonymous, 'Beautify Your Homes', *The Manufacturer and Builder*, December 1877, p. 283.

Anonymous, 'Books of the Week, review, *The Times*, 18 August 1892.

Anonymous, 'Character of Jefferson', *North American Review*, January 1835, 170–232.

Anonymous, 'Close of the Chelsea Flower Show', article, *The Times*, 23 May 1913.

Anonymous, 'Continuous Rails for Railways', *The Manufacturer and Builder*, December 1890, p. 274.

Anonymous, 'Cottage Design', *The Manufacturer and Builder*, October 1874, p. 236.

Anonymous, 'Design for a Villa', *The Manufacturer and Builder*, July 1869, p. 217.

Anonymous, 'Editor's Easy Chair', *Harper's New Monthly Magazine*, November 1859, page 841 (untitled report on Central Park progress).

Anonymous, 'Editor's easy Chair', *Harper's New Monthly Magazine*, September 1872, p. 620.

Anonymous, 'Farmers and Golfers', editorial, *The Times*, 6 December 1910.

Anonymous, 'Farmers and Golfers', news report, *The Times*, 5 December 1910.

Anonymous, 'German Home Life', *Living Age*, 4 September 1875, pp. 613–624.

Anonymous, 'Gloomy Return of an Old Foe: Moles in the Garden', article, *The Times*, 29 January 1968.

Anonymous, 'Hay Making at Home', article, *The Times*, 3 June 1943.

Anonymous, 'Home and Society', *Scribner's Monthly*, August 1872, pp 501–3.

Anonymous, 'Home and Society', *Scribner's Monthly*, July 1872, pp 372–3.

Anonymous, 'Home and Society', *Scribner's Monthly*, July 1874, p. 301–3.

Anonymous, 'Home and Society', *Scribner's Monthly*, June 1872, pp 246–7.

Anonymous, 'Improvements in the Parks', article, *The Times*, 29 September 1866.

Anonymous, 'Lawn Mower', *The Manufacturer and Builder*, May 1873, p. 115.

Anonymous, 'Machine Work in Gardens', article, *The Times*, 22 July 1916.

Anonymous, 'Mechanical Grass-Mowing', *The Manufacturer and Builder*, April 1874, p. 92.

Anonymous, *Monticello: A Guide for Visitors*. Charlottesville, Virginia: The Thomas Jefferson Foundation, n.d. (booklet).

Anonymous, *Monticello: The Flower Gardens*. Charlottesville, Virginia: The Thomas Jefferson Foundation, n.d. (leaflet).

Anonymous, 'Mortlake, the Hospital Farm Horse', news report, *The Times*, February 28, 1919.

Anonymous, 'Novel War Devices', article, *The Times*, 1 July 1918.

Anonymous, *Pavilion Gardens*. Charlottesville, Virginia: University of Virginia, n.d. (leaflet).

Anonymous, 'Penalties of Fame', *Scientific American* 10 (new series) (21), 325, 21 May 1864.

Anonymous, 'Prince Albert's Annual Sale of Livestock', article, *The Times*, 21 October 1841.

Anonymous, 'Public Walks', article, *The Times*, 7 September 1833.

Anonymous, 'Residence of a Country Physician', *The Manufacturer and Builder*, January 1890, p. 20.

Anonymous, review of the 'Proceedings and Report of the Commissioners for the University of Virginia', *North American Review*, January 1820, 115–137.

Anonymous, 'Summer on the Way', article, *The Times*, 5 May 1941.

Anonymous, 'Sun Flowers a Preventive of Fever and Ague', *Scientific American* 12 (37), 293, 23 May 1857.

Anonymous, 'The Editor's easy Chair', *Harper's New Monthly Magazine*, November 1859, p. 841.

Anonymous, 'The Great Exhibition', editorial, *The Times*, 24 April 1851.

Anonymous, 'The History of Hyde-Park', news report, *The Times*, 9 August 1866.

Anonymous, 'The Lawn and the Mower', editorial, *The Times*, 16 May 1945.

Anonymous, *The Rotunda*. Charlottesville, Virginia: University of Virginia, 2005 (leaflet).

Anonymous, 'The Seizure of Explosives', news report, *The Times*, 12 April 1883.

Anonymous, 'The Sheep and the Goats', article, *The Times*, 31 May 1926.

Anonymous, *Thomas Jefferson's Monticello*. Charlottesville, Virginia: The Thomas Jefferson Foundation, n.d. (leaflet).

Anonymous, 'To Mow or to Graze', article, *The Times*, 30 May 1944.

Anonymous, 'Trial of Mowing Machines', *Scientific American*, 26 July 1856, p. 366.

Anonymous, 'Under Trees and on the Water', article, *The Times*, 4 August 1916.

Anonymous, 'Vicar and Congregation', article, *The Times*, 21 December 1922.

Anonymous, 'Weeds and Seeds', article, *The Times*, 16 June 1930.

Anonymous, 'Weeds and Lawns', article, *The Times*, 10 September 1932.

Anonymous, 'Weeds on the Lawn', article, *The Times*, 31 May 1926.

Bagshaw F.A. (collated), *The home lawn* (1st ed.). Sydney: Division of Plant Industry, New South Wales Department of Agriculture, 1966.

Beale, Reginald, Book of the lawn: the making and maintenance of lawns and greens for all purposes. London: Cassell, 1931

Bormann, F. Herbert, Diana Balmori, Gordon T. Geballe, *Redesigning the American lawn: a search for environmental harmony*. New Haven: Yale University Press, c2001.

Carleton, R. Milton, *The New Way to Kill Weeds in Your Lawn and Garden*. New York: Arco Publishing Co Inc., 1957.

Carleton, R. Milton, *Your lawn, how to make it and keep it*. Princeton, N.J.: Van Nostrand, 1959.

Carruth, Hayden, 'A Suburban Adventure', *Harper's New Monthly Magazine*, 92, Issue 550, 645–654, 1896.

Chapman, G.P., *The biology of grasses*. Wallingford, Oxon, UK: CAB International, c1996.

Chester, K. Starr, *Nature and Prevention of Plant Diseases*. New York: McGraw-Hill, 1950.

City of East Lansing, *PACE: Parking & Code Enforcement*. http://www.cityofeastlansing.com/CITYGOV/PACE/Ordinances.asp, last viewed August 18, 2008.

City of New Berlin v. Hagar, No. 33582 (Wis. Cir. Ct. Waukesha Cty. Apr. 21, 1976).

Cornish, C.J., 'Outdoor Life in Holland', *Living Age*, 10 July 1897, p. 113–18.

Cunningham, Isabel Shipley, 'Frank Meyer, Agricultural Explorer', *Arnoldia* 44 (3), 1984, 3–26. See http://arnoldia.arboretum.harvard.edu/pdf/articles/1169.pdf, last viewed 21 August 2008.

Decker, Henry F., *Lawn care: a handbook for professionals*. Englewood Cliffs, N.J.: Prentice Hall, c1988.

Denning, Lord, MR [1977] QB 966, at 976, judgement in Miller vs Jackson.

Downing, A.J., *A Treatise on the Theory and Practise of Landscape Gardening*, 6th edition with a supplement by Henry Winthrop Sargent. New York, A. O. Moore and Co., 1859, available through http://books.google.com/books.

Dyson, Freeman, *Infinite in All Directions*. Harmondsworth: Penguin Books, 1989.

Flint, Anthony, *This land: the battle over sprawl and the future of America*. Baltimore, Md.: Johns Hopkins University Press, 2006.

Froude, J.A., *Oceana, or England and Her Colonies*. London : Longmans, Green and Co., 1886.

Fussell, Paul, *Class*. New York: Summit Books, 1983.

Goulton-Constable, J., 'Long Suffering', letter to the editor, *The Times*, 20 September 1875.

Halford, David G., *Old lawn mowers*. Princes Risborough: Shire, 1982.

Hampshire, Kristen, *Landscaping & Lawn Care*. Gloucester, Mass.: Quarry Books, 2007.

Hatch, Peter J., *The Gardens of Thomas Jefferson's Monticello*. Charlottesville, Virginia: The Thomas Jefferson Foundation, 1992.

Hawthorne, Nathaniel, 'A London Suburb', *The Atlantic Monthly*, 11, Issue 65, March 1863, 306–21.

Hay, Rob, 'Laying Down the Lawn', article, *The Times*, 13 April 1968.

Henning, Rachel, *The Letters of Rachel Henning*. Project Gutenberg: http://gutenberg.net.au/ebooks06/0607821.txt, last viewed 27 August 2008.

Henry, O., 'The Atavism of John Tom Little'. In *Selected Stories*, (ed. Guy Davenport), Harmondsworth: Penguin Classics, 1993.

Hessayon, D.G., *Be Your Own Lawn Expert*. Waltham Abbey: Pan Britannica Industries, 1961.

Hope, Jack, 'A Better Mousetrap', *American Heritage Magazine*, 47 (6), October 1996, accessed at http://www.americanheritage.com/articles/magazine/ah/1996/6/1996_6_90.shtml, last accessed 17 September, 2008.

Houghton, Albert Allison, *Molding concrete fountains and lawn ornaments.* N.Y., 1912.

Investigator, 'Sierra-Leone', letter to *The Times*, 4 January 1820.

Jenkins, Virginia Scott, *The Lawn: A History of an American Obsession.* Washington: Smithsonian Institution, 1994.

Laurie, Alex and Victor H. Ries, *Floriculture: Fundamentals and Practices.* New York: McGraw-Hill, 1942.

Lloyd, Nathaniel, 'Care of Golf Greens', letter to *The Times*, 12 March 1932.

Lowenfels, Jeff, *Teaming with microbes: a gardener's guide to the soil food web.* Portland, Or.: Timber Press, 2006.

Macinnis, Peter, *Mr Darwin's Incredible Shrinking World.* Sydney: Pier 9, 2008.

Macinnis, Peter, *The Killer Bean of Calabar and Other Stories.* Sydney: Allen and Unwin, 2004. (In the USA, *Poison.* New York: Arcade, 2005.)

Massey, F.P., Smith, M.J., Lambin X. and Hartley S.E., 'Are silica defences in grasses driving vole population cycles?' *Biology Letters*, 4 (4) 419–22, August 23, 2008 (published online, 15 May 2008: doi:10.1098/rsbl.2008.0106.

Maxwell, Sir Herbert, 'Links and Courses', letter to *The Times*, 1 December 1920.

Meisel, Paul, *Making lawn ornaments in wood.* East Petersburg, PA: Fox Books, c1999.

Montgomery County, Maryland v. Stewart, SW-87-2056 (Montgomery County, Md. Circuit Court, 1987).

Palin, Robert., *The master gardener's guide to lawn care.* London: Salamander, c1985.

Parfitt, David, *Lawnscapes: Mowing Patterns to Make Your Yard a Work of Art.* Philadelphia: Quirk Books, 2007.

Parkinson, C. Northcote, *British Intervention in Malaya.* Kuala Lumpur: University of Malaya Press, 1960.

Parsons, Samuel Jnr, 'Lawn-Planting for City and Country', *Scribner's Monthly*, 18 (2), 249–55.

Parsons, Samuel Jr., 'Lawn-Planting for Small Places', *Scribner's Monthly*, March 1879, p. 725–30.

Parsons, Samuel Jr., 'Village Lawn-Planting', *Scribner's Monthly*, May 1879, p. 48–56.

Playfair, Colonel W.M., 'Origin of Lawn Tennis', letter to *The Times*, 21 May 1927.

Prasad, Vandana, Strömberg, Caroline, Alimohammadian, Habib, Sahni, Ashok, 'Dinosaur coprolites and the early evolution of grasses and grazers'. *Science* 310: 1177–80, 2005.

Prisk, Max, 'Hands Across the Water', *Sydney Morning Herald*, 16–17 August 2008.

Ranney, Frances J., 'What's a Reasonable Woman to Do? The Judicial Rhetoric of Sexual Harassment'. *NWSA Journal* 9 (2), 1-22.

Robbins, Mary Caroline, 'The Art of Public Improvement', *The Atlantic Monthly*, 78, Issue 470, p. 747, 1896.

Robinson, W. (William), The wild garden. London: The Garden Office; New York: Scribner and Welford, 1881.

Rogers, Trey, *Lawn Geek*. New York: New American Library, 2007.

Schaechter, Moselio, *In the company of mushrooms: a biologist's tale*. Cambridge, Mass.: Harvard University Press, 1997.

Seale, Allan, *Allan Seale's Garden Book of Lawns and Ground Cover*. Balgowlah: Reed Books, 1985.

Senyard, June, *The tartan on University Square: a history of Victoria Bowling Club: 1876–2001*. Petersham, N.S.W.: Walla Walla Press, 2001.

Steinberg, Ted, American Green: *The Obsessive Quest for the Perfect Lawn*. New York: W.W. Norton, 2006.

Steinberg, Ted, *Down to Earth: Nature's Role in American History*. New York: Oxford University Press, 2002)

Teyssot, Georges (ed.), *The American Lawn*. New York: Princeton Architectural Press, 1999.

Thompson, Maurice, 'Bow Shooting'. *Scribner's Monthly*, July 1877, 277–8.

Thompson, Maurice, 'Merry Days with the Bow and Quiver', *Scribner's Monthly*, May 1878, pp. 1–16.

Tukey, Paul, *Organic Lawn Care Manual*. North Adams, Mass.: Storey Publishing, 2007.

Turner, Ethel, *Seven Little Australians*. Ringwood: Puffin Books, 2001.

'Uncle Charley', 'The Rules of Croquet II', *Scribner's Monthly*, October 1876, p. 906–7.

'Uncle Charley', 'The Rules of Croquet', *Scribner's Monthly*, August 1876, p. 597–8.

US Environmental Protection Agency, 'Green Landscaping with Native Plants:

Weed Laws', *John Marshall Law Review*, 26 (3), 1993. Available at http://www.
epa.gov/greenacres/weedlaws/JMLR.html

Vargas, J.M., Jr., *Management of turfgrass diseases* (2nd ed.). Boca Raton: Lewis
Publishers, c1994.

Veblen, Thorstein, *The theory of the leisure class: an economic study of institutions*.
New York: Macmillan, 1912.

Wainwright, Alexander, 'Lawn Tennis', *Scribner's Monthly*, August 1879, p.
624–6.

Whitman, Walt, *Song of Myself*, VI. Reprinted in *The Norton Anthology of Poetry*,
4th edition, 1996, p. 961 and numerous other anthologies.

Wilson, Jean, *Entertainment for Elizabeth I*. London: D. S. Brewer, 1980.

Wordsworth, William, *This Lawn a Carpet All Alive*. Published 1835.
Accessed online from http://www.everypoet.com/Archive/poetry/William_
Wordsworth/william_wordsworth_751.htm, last accessed 16 November, 2008.

Youngner, V.B. and C.M. McKell (eds), *The Biology and utilization of grasses*.
New York: Academic Press, 1972.

Yumlu, S.V., *Lawn mower use and emissions in Canada*. Ottawa, Ont.:
Environment Canada, 1994.

ACKNOWLEDGMENTS

I thank the lovely people at the State Library of NSW for having such excellent online databases that we card holders can access from home, the University of Sydney's Fisher Library and its branch libraries (especially Badham Library) for having such excellent collections, and Cornell University for having the 'Making of America' archive online. I have been a beta user of the Historic Australian Newspapers project at the National Library of Australia, and that also has been a handy source of the unexpected.

As usual, I wish to thank my friends at Upper Branches and Talk, many of whom went ABCD (above and beyond the call of duty) in digging for oddities and quirks relating to lawns. Julie Teague, Mike Pingleton, Pam North, Dee Churchill, Mary Pritchard, Sue Kamm, Lesley Knieriem, Debra Eisert, Pam McLaughlin, Rich Hansen, Robin Carroll-Mann, Jean Lowerison, Jackie Griffin, Marian Drabkin, Connie Jennings, Sue Watkins, MaryLou White, Dan Robinson, Sandy Schmitz, Mickey Laskin, Luke Long in the USA and Chris Corston in Canada (who told me about Paul Fussell), Sylvia Milne in the UK (who introduced me to Paxton) and Even Flood in Norway are all on one or the other of those lists.

Some of those named are also on the Project Wombat list of people who delight in burrowing for information. Adrian Smith of Leeds is also on PW: he provided me with handy patent advice. On the same list, Michele Jack found two possible candidates for the active ingredient in 'Carter's Worm Killer': nicotine and anhydrous ammonia fertiliser, but the mystery remains open.

Katy Murray at the Royal Parks in London provided some background on park sheep which not only answered my questions but sent me off in useful directions. My older son Angus pointed me to places where I could extract useful court cases and introduced me to Denning's views on 'The Cricket Case' while my younger son Duncan spied out lawns in Cambridge for me. My daughter Cate provided ecological advice and my wife Chris patiently read the manuscript several times.

John Ahern in Townsville told me about Ercildoun, and Surrey Jacobs at the National Herbarium reminded me of some taxonomy basics that I had forgotten, and told me some detail that I never knew.

This book is my second collaboration with editor Shelley Kenigsberg, the first being *Mr Darwin's Incredible Shrinking World*, so like my family, Shelley is now more than usually familiar with the year 1859. Once again, Shelley has persuaded me to pay closer attention at many points to sloppy expression, though in her defence, I argued that one or two of these to stand on the ground that the apparent infelicities were features, not bugs. My thanks to Shelley, and also to Diana Hill, my publisher, who fed me lots of ideas and worked hard as a one-person encouragement and support team.

I would like to thank Reuben Crossman and the other talented artistic people who worked on my manuscript for their spectacular designs.

Lastly, my thanks to my granddaughter Brianna Ng, who showed me that there is more than one way to roll grass.

INDEX

A

Abel, Alan 195–6
Africa 46–7
agriculture 18–19, 29, 43, 61, 66, 67, 160–1, 180
Alice in Wonderland 206
animals 37–42, 88, 91–2, 132, 143 *see also* livestock
ants 140
archery 208–9
asthma 50, 109
Astor, J.J. 199
astroturf 90–1, 229
Austen, Jane 55–6

B

badminton 204
Balfour, Arthur 217
bamboo 34, 35
Banks, Joseph 92
baseball fields 123, 205, 217
Beale, Reginald 123–6, 137, 139, 140, 170, 213, 226
Beeton, Mrs 210
Bennis, Warren 74–5
biodiversity 113, 226
biological controls 131–2
birds 43, 85–8, 132, 139–40
the block 96
Boadicea 175
Bohr, Niels 12
Botany Bay 92
bowling greens 57, 104, 105
British colonies 60, 92, 94–6, 105
British Royal family 33, 58, 64, 64–5, 92, 223
Brown, Capability 58

Brown, Sarah 58, 59
Budding, Edwin 13, 17, 18, 157, 161
Bush, George W. 228

C

Carroll, Lewis 130, 206
Carruth, Hayden 171
Carson, Rachel 142, 229
Carthage 149
celebrities 101–5
cereal rusts 148
chemicals 43, 135–48, 150
Chicago's Riverside 51–4, 59, 66, 68
children 165, 211
Chile saltpetre 150–1
China, People's Republic of 10, 130, 228–9
Churchill, Winston 96, 141
Clarke, Arthur C. 12
Class (Fussell) 97
climate change 232
clovers 43, 111, 150
Cochrane, Thomas 149, 230
Columbus 126
Communist banner 61
Cook, James 92
coprolites 37, 38, 39–42
Cosby, Bill 75
crab-grass 132, 142, 145
cricket 186, 205, 221–3
croquet lawn 93, 94, 144, 164–5, 204, 205–9, 216
Crystal Palace (London) 59, 60, 71

D

Darwin awards 184
Darwin, Charles 12, 42, 113, 142, 226
Davy, Humphrey 150
Denning, Lord 221–3
Denver, John 181
Dickens, Charles 12, 104–5
Diderot, Denis 30
dinosaurs 37, 38–42, 71
disease 46–8, 50, 141, 211
Downing, Andrew 66–8, 73, 106, 227
Drake, Sir Francis 57
drought 85, 226–7, 229, 232

E

earthworms 137–9, 142
eelworms 131
Elizabeth I, Queen 200
Emerson, Ralph Waldo 187
ergot 145–8
Eton's playing fields 201
Eucalypts 37–8, 47, 122

F

farmers 45–6, 61, 78, 107, 161
fast food 50
Federer, Roger 230–1
Ferrabee, John 17, 170
fertilisers 149–51, 227
field hockey 186, 230
fire 48, 54, 78, 82, 109
Fisher, Henry 161–2
Fitzgerald, F. Scott 50–1, 108
Fleming, John 16
flint sickles 61

football 201, 204, 217–20
fossil grasses 37
France 30, 69
Franklin, Benjamin 69
Fraser, Sir William 201
Froude, J.A. 93–4, 114–15
fuel 34, 176, 180, 225, 228, 232
fungicides 143
Furphy, Joseph 94
Fussell, Paul 97

G
Gallipoli 96
garden parties 106
Gavin, Jim 188
gender 27, 46, 76–8, 122, 178, 182–5, 205
genealogy 105
Germany 19–20, 155
golf courses 36, 126, 142–3, 204
golf links 214–16
Gondwana 37, 42
Google Earth 20–1
grain crops 34
grass dyes 130
grass forests 35
grass-roots politics 90–1, 106
grasses *see also* lawn grasses: as anarchists 27–8, 121, 232; botanical names 31, 34–5; evolution and 37–43; as flowering plants 18, 39, 112; native 93; nature of 31–5, 36; seeds 126, 128–9; as stockfeed 92
grasslands 82
grave grasses 128

greenhouses 60, 127
greenkeepers 214
guano 150–1
Gutenberg, Johannes 11–12

H
ha-ha 57
Hagar, Donald 109
Hampton Court 58, 197
Hawthorne, Nathaniel 104
hay 19, 34, 114–15
heavy metals 139
hedgerow 91
Hemings, Sally 68–9
Hemingway, Ernest 51
Henning, Rachel 93
Herbert, Spencer 42
Hessayon, David 100
hockey 186, 230
home turf 46
hothouses 59
hunters 45–6, 78
Husqvarna 177
Hyde Park 60, 64–5, 114, 210, 211

I
ice hockey 201
improvement 55–6, 58, 106–7, 171
India 37, 39, 201
insecticides 140–2
internet 12–13, 76
Ireland 105, 155, 204
Irving, Washington 70

J
Japan 31

Japanese maples 71
Jefferson, Thomas 68–70
John Deere 180, 188

K
Kingsley, Charles 201

L
landscaping 54, 58, 59, 71, 74
Lantana 132
the law 76–7, 83–4, 143, 184, 214–16, 221, 221–3; weed ordinances 108–12, 115
lawn: as an alien concept 26–7; in city and country 71; cost of 29–30, 177, 225, 226–32; defending 117–21, 124; exclusionary 115; future of 226–32; inedibility of 61, 103; lawnsman's art 121–30; mavericks 108–15; nationalism 19–21, 26, 50; needs 150–1; notable examples 21, 31, 69–70, 106; as a symbol 106; tree plantings and 107; ubiquity of 31; unified 68
lawn billiards 204
lawn bowls 57, 104, 105, 230
lawn cemetary 87, 96–7
lawn clippings 143–4, 227
lawn deer 202–3
lawn games 199–209, 220
lawn grasses *see also* lawn plants: breeding 126, 128; buffalo grass 93–4, 118, 129, 231; cultivars 123, 231; English grass 115, 126; grass transfers

126–8; Kentucky bluegrass 71, 109, 123; kikuyu grass 126–7; naming 122; species 81, 82, 114, 126–7, 145
'lawn' in rhyme 95
lawn jockeys 196–7
lawn mower: acceptance of 157; accidents 178–85; advertisers 141, 164–70, 182–3, 185–6; cylinder 17, 160, 177; electric 186; emissions 225; fitted with GPS 178; fuel consumption of 225, 228; grass catchers 227; as a hedge trimmer 184; invention of 8, 10, 13, 17; manual push mower 16; manufacture of 228; models 74, 78, 160–3, 164–70, 180; powered 174–90; races 188–9; reel 160–3; repairs 170; ride-on 180, 184; robot 177–8; rotary 177, 181; steam-powered 174–5; in war cemeteries 96–7
lawn mowing 46–51, 74–8, 113–14, 115, 132
lawn ornaments 193–7, 202–3
lawn pets 195
lawn plants 31, 35–6, 57, 95, 231 see also lawn grasses
lawn pool 209
lawn porn 185
lawn puns 210
Lawn Rangers 189
lawn rollers 176, 177, 180, 186–7
lawn service 75–6, 184–5, 227–8
lawn teas 206
lawn tennis 94, 156–7, 199–200, 204, 209, 216–19 see also tennis courts
leather-jackets 140
leisure class 28–9, 30
leisure time 8, 9, 17
Lewis, John 16–17
Linnaeus, Carl 35, 113
literature and lawns 94–7, 101–2, 171
livestock 29, 30, 51–4, 57, 65, 92, 195, 211; horses 114, 150, 160, 173–4, 210; sheep 60–1, 66, 73, 114, 156
Lloyd, Nathaniel 139–40
LSD 145
luxury lawns 100, 103

M
McDonalds 50
Mackellar, Dorothy 82, 95

McLuhan, Marshall 12
Magnus, Albertus 18
Maher, Bill 76
Manet, Edouard 210
Mansfield, Lord 55
Mansfield Park (Austen) 55–6
Marie Antoinette 32–3, 68, 178
Mark Twain 76
Marshall, Thurgood 75
Martin, Charles 84
Marx Brothers 75
Maxwell, Herbert 215–16
meadow and pasture 9, 27, 64–5
medicinal plants 132
medieval Europe 18, 34
Meisel, Paul 193
Melbourne Cup 204
Meyer, Frank N 127–8
Meyer Zoysia 128
miasmas 48, 210
microarthropods 143–4
Middle East 61
moles 139, 146–7
Monet, Claude 210
monocultures 42–3, 130–1
Monsanto 229
Monticello 69–70
mosquitoes 47, 141
moss 31, 144
motor vehicles 174
mountain ash 122
mountain climbing 201
mow 9, 17
mowing see also agriculture; lawn mowing: by animals 156–7, 167, 174; horse-drawn 160, 173–4; by sheep 60–1, 66, 73, 114, 156; the shoulder 91–2
'My Country' (Mackellar) 95

N
Nadal, Rafael 230–1
Naples (Italy) 141
napping shears 15–17
Native Americans 76, 115
nature, dominance and control over 27–8
nematodes 131
the Netherlands 20, 54
New York's Central Park 13, 59–60, 66–7, 71, 73, 209
New Zealand 60, 89, 93, 95
nitrogen 43, 111, 150
nitroglycerine 155–6
Nixon, Richard 106
Nobel Prize 142

nouveau riche 55–6
noxious weeds 112, 127

O
O Henry 76
official lawns 106
Olympic Games 10, 130, 189, 228–9, 231
open space 8, 13, 107
opium poppy 113
O'Rourke, P.J. 145

P
the paddock 92
park ideal 66–7
parks see private parks; public parks
Parsons Jnr, Samuel 71–4
Paspalum notatum 127, 145
patents 160, 162–4
Paxton, Joseph 58–60
penguins 127
penicillin 142
pest control 130–2
pesticides 129, 131, 228
Phillip, Governor 92
phosphorus 150
photography 103, 119
phytoliths 38, 39–42
picnics 209–11
plant cuttings 127–8
plastic bottles on lawns 88
playing fields 10, 46, 123, 151, 201, 221
poachers 55, 113
poison sprays 129, 131, 228
polo clubs 201
potassium 150
Prasad, Vandana 37
printing press 11–12
Prior, George 142–3
Privacy (yacht) 221
private lawns 30
private parks 18, 58, 59–61 see also public parks
private property 89
professions 107–8
psychology 27–8, 61, 78, 97
public lawns 30–1, 66–7
public parks 30, 54–6, 59–61, 64–7, 71–4, 114, 119–20, 209–11
public property 89
public transport 8–9, 13, 53, 54, 74
putting green 214, 215, 226

Q
quarter-acre block 96

R
rabbits 113, 131, 156–7
railways 13, 54
Ransome, Arthur 180
Reagan, Ronald P. 74
Red Cross 66
Regent's Park 17, 64, 65, 113, 175
Reynolds, Malvina 27–8, 232
rhizomes 36
rice 85–8
Richardson, Mervyn Victor 188
rickets 211
Riis, Jacob 119–20
roadkill 91–2
robot mowers 177–8
Rogers, Trey 153–4
Rome 34, 149, 175
the rub 57
ryegrass 36, 145–8

S
salt 149–50
savannahs 82
scarlet pimpernel 114–15
Scott Fitzgerald, F. 50–1, 108
scythe 17, 18, 48–9, 57, 61, 63–4, 78, 154–5, 157, 179
seed companies 123, 128–9, 137–9
seeds 34, 114–15, 126, 128–9, 132
self-sufficiency 108–9
Serling, Rod 181
Seven Little Australians (Turner) 49–50
Shakespeare, William 17–18, 57
Shanks, Alexander 160, 174
shaving and beards 112–14
ships 13, 60, 115
sickles 61
The Silent Spring (Carson) 142, 229
silica 38, 39 see also phytoliths
slaves 55, 68–9
slime moulds 148
snakes 48
social class 28–9, 55–6, 74–8, 82, 97, 115, 119
social effects of technology 11–13
Society for Indecency to Naked Animals 195–6
Solander, Daniel 92

Somersett, James 55
Spanish Main 126
spectator sports 216–32
sports, origins of 11, 46, 200–1, 231
springtails 144
sprinklers 227
status and authority 8, 9, 30–1, 76, 100–8
Stowe, Harriet Beecher 206
string trimmer 155
suburbs 8–9, 46, 51–4, 66, 112, 227
sugar cane 55, 126
summer-grass 132, 145
Sumner, James 174
sun flowers 48
sundials 104–5
synthetic surfaces 229–31

T
tanks 179
technologies 11–13
television 228–31
tennis courts 36, 57, 93, 111, 137, 213, 230–1 see also lawn tennis
Tennyson, Alfred 103
textiles industry 14–17
Thailand 198
The Times 199
topiary 197–8
trace elements 151
tractors 174
transportation 113
trespass 83
tuberculosis 211
turf 31, 34, 71, 129–30, 131, 153–4, 229
Turner, Ethel 49–50

U
United States: Civil War 196–7, 205; in Middle East 26
universities 70–1, 118, 151, 170
USSR 61
utility lawns 100, 106, 174

V
van Gogh, Vincent 120–1
Vaux, Calvert 59–60, 66–7, 71
Veblen, Thorstein 28–9, 30, 103, 195
vegetable garden 103, 106, 108–9
verge 89, 91–2
Victa mower 10, 188, 189

Victoria, Queen 59, 201
voles 39

W
war cemeteries 96–7
Warringah Golf Club 143
Washington, George 57, 196
Washington Mall 106, 127, 223–4
water turf 230
water wars 231, 232
watering 82, 85, 130, 226–7
weeds 36, 114, 132, 135, 140, 145–8; weed ordinances 108–12
Wellington, Duke of 201
West Indies 55, 93
White House lawn 60, 66, 106
Whitman, Walt 95
wild lawns 109–15
wildlife 91–2
Wimbledon 204, 216–17
Woodrow Wilson, Thomas 60, 66
Woods, Tiger 221
Wordsworth, William 74, 102–3
World War I 96, 176, 179
World War II 31, 113–14, 141, 156, 176
Wright brothers 12

X
xeriscaped surfaces 231–2

Z
Zoysia genus 128

First published in 2009 by Pier 9, an imprint of Murdoch Books Pty Limited

Murdoch Books Australia
Pier 8/9
23 Hickson Road
Millers Point NSW 2000
Phone: +61 (0)2 8220 2000
Fax: +61 (0)2 8220 2558
www.murdochbooks.com.au

Murdoch Books UK Limited
Erico House, 6th Floor
93–99 Upper Richmond Road
Putney, London SW15 2TG
Phone: +44 (0)20 8785 5995
Fax: +44 (0)20 8785 5985
www.murdochbooks.co.uk

Publisher: Diana Hill
Project Manager: Paul O'Beirne
Design: Reuben Crossman

Text copyright © Peter Macinnis
The moral right of the author has
been asserted.

Design copyright © Murdoch Books
Pty Limited 2009

National Library of Australia
Cataloguing-in-Publication Data:
Author: Macinnis, P. (Peter)
Title: The Lawn: A Social History /
Peter Macinnis
ISBN: 9781741960396 (pbk.)
Notes: Includes index.
Bibliography.
Subjects: Lawns—history.
Social history.
Dewey Number: 635.9647

Image credits
Alamy: p 182
Clipart.com: p 190
Corbis: pp 6, 52, 72, 219
iStockphoto: front cover, pp 5, 79,
86, 110, 125, 133, 146, 202, 224, 233
Photolibrary: pp 22–23, 32, 40, 41,
166, 191
The Picture Desk: pp 158–159, 218

Text credit
Every reasonable effort has been
made to trace the owners of copyright
materials in this book, but is some
instances this has proven impossible.
The author(s) and publisher will be
glad to receive information leading to
more complete acknowledgments in
subsequent printings of the book and
in the meantime extend their apologies
for any omissions.

Page 28: *God Bless the Grass*,
M. Reynolds © 1964 Schroder Music
Company. Used by permission of
Schroder Music Company.

A catalogue record for this book is
available from the British Library.

Printed by C&C Offset Printing Co.
Ltd in 2009. Printed in China.